WHAT WAS THE INTERTESTAMENTAL PERIOD?

Kids' Guides to God's Word Series

What Is the Book of Genesis?
What Is the Book of Exodus?
What Is the Book of Leviticus?
What Is the Book of Numbers?
What Is the Book of Deuteronomy?
What Is the Book of Joshua?
What Is the Book of Judges?
What Is the Book of Ruth?
What Is the Book of 1 Samuel?
What Is the Book of 2 Samuel?
What Is the Book of 1 Kings?
What Is the Book of 2 Kings?
What Are the Books of 1–2 Chronicles?
What Are the Books of Ezra & Nehemiah?
What Is the Book of Esther?
What Is the Book of Job?
What Is the Book of Psalms?
What Is the Book of Proverbs?
What Is the Book of Ecclesiastes?
What Are the Books of Song of Songs & Lamentations?
What Is the Book of Isaiah?
What Is the Book of Jeremiah?
What Is the Book of Ezekiel?
What Is the Book of Daniel?
What Are the Books of Hosea–Micah?
What Are the Books of Nahum–Malachi?

What Is the Gospel of Matthew?
What Is the Gospel of Mark?
What Is the Gospel of Luke?
What Is the Gospel of John?
What Is the Book of Acts?
What Is the Book of Romans?
What Is the Book of 1 Corinthians?
What Is the Book of 2 Corinthians?
What Is the Book of Galatians?
What Is the Book of Ephesians?
What Is the Book of Philippians?
What Are the Books of Colossians & Philemon?
What Are the Books of 1–2 Thessalonians?
What Are the Books of 1–2 Timothy & Titus?
What Is the Book of Hebrews?
What Is the Book of James?
What Are the Books of 1–2 Peter & Jude?
What Are the Books of 1-3 John?
What Is the Book of Revelation?

What Was the
INTERTESTAMENTAL PERIOD?

Michael Whitworth

ISBN 978-1-971767-41-3

Published by Start2Finish
Bend, Oregon 97702
start2finish.org

Printed in the United States of America
30 29 28 27 26   1 2 3 4 5

CONTENTS

INTRODUCTION

Have you ever started watching a TV show in the middle of a season? Everyone on screen already knows each other. They're arguing about something that happened three episodes ago. They reference people you've never met. They're dealing with consequences of events you didn't see. And you're sitting there thinking: *What did I miss? Who are these people? Why does everyone seem so upset?*

That's almost exactly what it feels like to turn from the last page of the Old Testament to the first page of the New.

When the Old Testament ends, the temple is a modest rebuilt structure. When Matthew opens, it's been transformed by Herod into the largest sacred complex in the ancient world.

When the Old Testament ends, the Jewish people are a tiny community under Persian rule. When the New Testament begins, they're scattered across the Roman Empire with synagogues in every major city.

When Malachi finishes prophesying, there are no Pharisees, no Sadducees, no scribes, no Sanhedrin. When Jesus starts teaching, these groups are everywhere, and everyone seems to know who they are and what they stand for.

Something happened. Something enormous. And most people have no idea what it was.

THE GAP NOBODY TALKS ABOUT

Open most Bibles and you'll find a blank page between Malachi and Matthew. Maybe two. That's it. That tiny gap represents roughly four hundred years of history, and most people skip right past it without a second thought. They call it "the 400 years of silence," as if God took a long nap between the Testaments and woke up just in time for the birth of Jesus.

That label is misleading. These four centuries were anything but silent. They were some of the most dramatic, turbulent, and consequential years in the history of God's people. Empires rose and fell. The Jewish homeland was conquered, fought over, and reshaped. A Greek conqueror changed the language of the entire world. A family of Jewish rebels took up swords and won their freedom against impossible odds. A paranoid king rebuilt the temple on a scale that staggered the imagination and then murdered his own family to keep his throne. New ideas about resurrection, final judgment, and the coming of a Messiah took shape and became the framework for everything the New Testament would teach.

And through all of it, God was at work. Not through prophets, as he had been in the Old Testament. The prophetic voice did go quiet after Malachi. But God's hand kept moving through providence, through the rise and fall of nations, through the quiet faithfulness of ordinary people, and through circumstances that no one at the time could fully understand. He was preparing the world for something no one saw coming.

This book is about what happened in that gap. And once you know the story, you'll never read the New Testament the same way again.

WHAT YOU'RE ABOUT TO READ

Here's where we're headed.

We'll start where the Old Testament leaves off, with the Jewish people back in their land after the Babylonian exile, rebuilding their temple, clinging to the law of Moses, and waiting for God to finish what he started. The promises of a coming king, a restored kingdom, and a world made right are still hanging in the air, unfulfilled.

Then the world turns upside down. A young Greek prince named Alexander conquers everything from Greece to India, and Greek language and culture flood the ancient world. The Jewish people find themselves caught between two rival empires, squeezed and taxed and fought over like a bone between two dogs. The pressure to abandon their faith and become Greek intensifies until a Seleucid king named Antiochus decides to erase Jewish identity altogether. He outlaws their religion, desecrates their temple, and forces them to choose between their faith and their lives.

A family of priests picks up swords and fights back. The Maccabean revolt is one of the most astonishing stories you've never heard: a band of guerrilla fighters taking on the most powerful empire in the eastern Mediterranean and winning. They rededicate the temple, establish an independent Jewish kingdom for the first time in centuries, and prove that faith can survive even the most brutal assault.

But independence doesn't solve everything. The dynasty that rises from the Maccabees becomes corrupt. Rome arrives and swallows the region whole. A half-Jewish tyrant named Herod takes the throne. And the Jewish nation fractures into competing factions: Pharisees, Sadducees, Essenes, and violent revolutionaries known as Zealots, each with a different vision of what faithfulness looks like.

Meanwhile, a new way of worshiping takes shape. Synagogues spring up across the known world, putting Scripture into the hands and ears of ordinary people every week. The Bible is translated into Greek. Teachers and scribes become the new spiritual authorities. And through it all, the hope for a Messiah burns hotter and hotter until, by the time a baby is born in Bethlehem, expectation is at a fever pitch.

That's the story of the intertestamental period. It's the bridge between the two halves of your Bible. And every bit of it matters.

WHY THIS MATTERS FOR YOU

You might be thinking: *That's interesting, but it happened over two thousand years ago. Why should I care?*

Because you can't understand the New Testament without it. When Jesus walks into a synagogue and reads from the scroll of Isaiah, you need to know where synagogues came from. When the Pharisees challenge him about Sabbath rules, you need to know why they cared so much about those rules. When Pontius Pilate washes his hands and Rome crucifies the

Son of God, you need to understand how Rome got there and what it meant for a Jewish man to be executed by a pagan empire. When the early church spreads across the Mediterranean world using Greek language, Roman roads, and the synagogue network, you need to see that God spent four hundred years building the infrastructure for that moment.

The intertestamental period isn't a gap in the story. It's the setup for the greatest event in human history.

BEFORE YOU BEGIN

A couple of things to keep in mind as you read.

This book is different from the others in this series. Every other book walks through a specific book of the Bible, chapter by chapter. This one doesn't, because there is no single biblical book that covers this period. Instead, we're covering about four hundred years of history, organized by topic and era. You'll still find the same structure in each chapter: an opening hook, the historical content, application, and discussion questions. But the content itself moves through time rather than through a text.

Some of the history is violent. Wars, massacres, persecution, political murder. The intertestamental period was not gentle, and this book doesn't pretend it was. The Jewish people endured extraordinary suffering during these centuries, and understanding that suffering is part of understanding who they were when Jesus arrived.

Finally, this is ultimately a story about God's faithfulness. Four hundred years is a long time to wait. Generations were born and died without seeing the fulfillment of what the prophets had promised. But God never forgot. He never stopped working. And when the time was exactly right, he kept every promise he had ever made. As Paul wrote, "When the fullness of time had come, God sent forth his Son…" (Galatians 4:4).

So let's go back to where the Old Testament ends, to a tiny community of Jewish people huddled behind rebuilt walls in a rebuilt city, reading the law of a God who had rescued them from Babylon and wondering what he would do next.

The answer is bigger than they could have imagined.

Turn the page.

1

NOT REALLY SILENT

Arthur Conan Doyle wrote a Sherlock Holmes mystery called "Silver Blaze" about a famous racehorse that disappears the night before a big race. Holmes is called in to investigate. At the end, when he reveals who took the horse, a detective asks if there was any particular clue that cracked the case. Holmes points to "the curious incident of the dog in the night-time."

The detective is confused. "The dog did nothing in the night-time."

"That was the curious incident," Holmes replies.

The silence was the clue. A guard dog should have barked when someone came to steal the horse. The fact that it didn't bark told Holmes everything he needed to know: the intruder wasn't a stranger. It was someone the dog recognized. What looked like nothing happening was actually the most important piece of evidence in the entire case.

Most people think the period between the Old and New Testaments was like that dog: silent and uneventful. They call it "the 400 years of silence," as if God hung up the phone after the prophet Malachi and didn't call back until an angel appeared in Zechariah's temple at the start of Luke's Gospel. Pick up most timelines of Bible history, and you'll find a big blank space between the last page of the Old Testament and the first page of the New. Four centuries of—nothing?

Not even close.

The period between the Testaments wasn't empty at all. It was one of the most dramatic, turbulent, and important stretches of time in the entire biblical story. Empires rose and fell. The Jewish people were conquered, scattered, and nearly wiped out. New ideas emerged that would shape everything about the world Jesus was born into. And through all of it, every war, every crisis, every cultural earthquake, God was at work. Not through prophets, as he had been for centuries. The prophetic voice did go quiet after Malachi. But God's hand never stopped moving. He worked through providence, through the rise and fall of nations, through circumstances no one at the time could fully understand.

To see what happened in those four centuries, we need to start where the Old Testament actually ends. And it doesn't end with silence. It ends with expectation.

WHERE THE STORY STOOD

The Old Testament doesn't end the way most people think it does. If you've read through Genesis to Malachi, the story isn't wrapped up in a neat bow. It's more like a song that stops in the middle of a note. Everything is hanging.

Here's where things stood. About six hundred years before Jesus was born, the people of Judah had been conquered by the Babylonians. Jerusalem was destroyed. The temple, the place where God's presence dwelt among his people, was burned to the ground. The survivors were dragged into exile in Babylon. It was the worst disaster in Israel's history.

But the exile didn't last forever. In 539 BC, a Persian king named Cyrus conquered Babylon and issued an astonishing decree: the Jewish exiles could go home. They could rebuild their temple. They could start over.

And they did. A leader named Zerubbabel, who was a descendant of King David, led the first group of exiles back to Jerusalem. A priest named Joshua came with him. Together, with encouragement from the prophets Haggai and Zechariah, they rebuilt the temple. It was completed in 515 BC.

That temple, called the Second Temple, would stand for almost six hundred years, all the way into the time of Jesus. It became the center of Jewish life and worship. But it wasn't what it used to be. The older people who remembered Solomon's original temple wept when they saw the new one. It was smaller. It was less impressive. And the ark of the covenant—the gold-covered chest that represented God's throne among his people—was gone. It had disappeared when the Babylonians destroyed the first temple, and it never came back.

The temple was standing, but something was missing.

THE LAW TAKES CENTER STAGE

About a generation after the temple was rebuilt, a priest and scribe named Ezra arrived in Jerusalem from Babylon. Ezra was a scholar, a man devoted to studying the law of Moses and teaching it to others. He brought with him something that would reshape Jewish life forever: a fierce commitment to Scripture.

Before the exile, Israel's spiritual life had been driven by three kinds of leaders: priests who ran the temple, prophets who spoke for God, and kings who governed the nation. But now the kings were gone. The Davidic line had no political power. The last prophets were fading from the scene. And the priests, while still important, needed something to anchor the people's faith in a world that kept trying to pull them away from God.

That anchor was the law of Moses, the first five books of the Bible.

Ezra gathered the people in Jerusalem and read the law to them publicly. He didn't just read it. He explained it, made sure they understood it, and called them to obey it. The people wept when they heard it. Many of them had never really listened to it before. Ezra also confronted a serious problem: many Jewish men had married women from surrounding nations who worshiped other gods. He insisted that the community purify itself, drawing a sharp line between God's people and the nations around them.

This was a turning point. From this moment forward, the Jewish people became known as a people of the Book. The law wasn't just a historical document. It was the blueprint for life. Studying it, teaching it, and obeying it became the defining features of what it meant to be a faithful Jew. And when the prophetic voice eventually went silent, it was Scripture that filled the space. God had already spoken. His words were written down. The people would cling to those words for centuries.

WALLS AND WARNINGS

Around the same time as Ezra, a man named Nehemiah arrived from Persia to tackle a different problem. Jerusalem was vulnerable. Its walls were still in ruins from the Babylonian invasion, which meant the city was exposed to enemies and raiders. Without walls, the community couldn't thrive.

Nehemiah organized the people to rebuild the walls despite fierce opposition from neighboring leaders who didn't want Jerusalem to become strong again. In just fifty-two days, the walls were up. It was an astonishing achievement, and it gave the small Jewish community the physical security it needed to survive.

But physical walls couldn't fix spiritual problems. The prophet Malachi, likely living around this same general period, delivered the last prophetic message recorded in the Old Testament. And it wasn't a comfortable one.

Malachi confronted the people and their priests for cutting corners in their worship. They were offering sick and injured animals as sacrifices (the leftovers nobody wanted) instead of the best of their flocks. The priests were supposed to be spiritual leaders, but they had grown lazy and careless. People were cheating on their tithes, breaking their marriage covenants, and wondering aloud whether serving God was even worth the effort.

"Where is the God of justice?" they asked (Malachi 2:17). In other words: if God is real, why isn't he doing anything?

Malachi's answer was pointed. God *was* going to act. A messenger would come to prepare the way. Then the Lord himself would suddenly appear at his temple. "But who can endure the day of his coming?" Malachi warned. God would come as a refiner's fire, purifying his people, judging the wicked, and vindicating those who feared his name. The last words of Malachi's prophecy looked forward to the return of Elijah before "the great and dreadful day of the Lord."

And then the prophetic voice went quiet.

THE PROMISES STILL HANGING

When the last prophet stopped speaking, it wasn't because everything was resolved. The voice went quiet right in the middle of the tension. Think about what was still unfinished when Malachi's prophecy ended.

God had promised David that one of his descendants would sit on an eternal throne. No one was sitting on that throne. Zerubbabel, who was from David's line, had led the return from exile, but he never became king. His descendants faded from public life. By the time a generation or two had passed, the house of David had no political power at all.

God had promised through the prophets that Israel would be restored. Not just brought back from exile, but truly restored. A united kingdom. Freedom from foreign rule. The nations streaming to Jerusalem to worship the God of Israel. None of that had happened. The Jewish people were back in their land, yes, but they were a tiny community under Persian control. They weren't free. They weren't united. They weren't anything close to what the prophets had described.

The temple was standing, but it lacked the glory of Solomon's temple. There was no ark of the covenant. There was no visible, overwhelming presence of God filling the building the way it had in the old days.

The law was being taught, but the people kept drifting. Malachi's prophecy made that painfully clear.

Everything God had promised was still out there, unclaimed. The question hanging over the end of the Old Testament isn't "Is the story over?" It's "When will God finish what he started?"

NOT SILENCE, BUT PROVIDENCE

That's the world we're stepping into. And here's what you need to understand before we go further: the four hundred years between Malachi and Jesus were not empty. They were not wasted. They were not a gap in the story.

God was at work. He wasn't sending prophets, and he wasn't performing the kind of dramatic, visible miracles that marked the days of Moses and Elijah. But he was moving, quietly and purposefully, through the events of history. He was arranging the pieces of a puzzle so enormous that no one alive at the time could have seen the full picture.

During these centuries, the Persian Empire gave way to the Greek Empire, and the Greek language spread across the known world, the very language in which the New Testament would be written. The Jewish Scriptures were translated into Greek so that people everywhere could read them. The synagogue system developed, so that by the time Jesus walked into a synagogue in Nazareth and opened a scroll, there were synagogues in every Jewish community from Jerusalem to Rome. The Roman Empire built roads connecting the entire Mediterranean world, roads that missionaries would one day use to carry the gospel from city to city.

New religious groups emerged: Pharisees, Sadducees, Essenes, and others, each wrestling with what it meant to be faithful to God in an increasingly complicated world. Messianic hope didn't die during these centuries. It intensified. By the time Jesus was born, expectation was running so hot that people were scanning the horizon for any sign that God was finally about to act.

None of this was coincidence. None of it was random. God wasn't silent. He was sovereign. He was working through events, through empires, through the decisions of kings and scholars and ordinary people who had no idea they were part of a plan set in motion before the foundation of the world.

The prophets had gone quiet. But the God who sent the prophets had not.

WHAT THIS MEANS FOR US

First, silence doesn't mean absence. When God stops speaking in obvious ways, it's tempting to think he's gone. The Jewish people lived for four hundred years without a prophetic voice, and many of them must have wondered if God had forgotten his promises. He hadn't. He was working in ways they couldn't see and wouldn't understand until the full picture came together. If you're in a season where God feels distant or quiet, that doesn't mean he's abandoned you. It may mean he's doing something too big for you to see right now.

Second, God's promises don't expire. Four hundred years is a long time to wait. Generations were born and died without seeing the fulfillment of what the prophets had spoken. But not one word of those promises fell to the ground. Every single one was kept, on God's timetable, not ours. When God makes a promise, the clock doesn't matter. He finishes what he starts, even if it takes longer than we think it should.

Third, God works through ordinary events. There were no parting seas or fire from heaven during these four centuries. God worked through political decisions, cultural shifts, and the rise and fall of empires. He used pagan kings and Greek philosophers and Roman road builders—none of whom were trying to serve him—to set the stage for the coming of his Son. God doesn't need miracles to accomplish his purposes. He's just as powerful in the ordinary as he is in the spectacular.

Fourth, preparation matters even when it doesn't feel productive. The Jewish people during this period were doing unglamorous things: studying Scripture, building synagogues, preserving their identity under foreign rule, teaching their children the faith. None of it looked dramatic. All of it mattered. When Jesus arrived, there was a people ready to hear him, a language for the gospel to be preached in, and a network of communities where the message could take root. The quiet, faithful work of ordinary people across four centuries made all of that possible.

TALKING POINTS

1. **Most people call the period between the Old and New Testaments "the 400 years of silence."** After reading this chapter, why do you think that label is misleading? What was actually happening during this time?

2. **Ezra brought a renewed focus on Scripture to the Jewish community after the exile.** Why do you think the law

of Moses became so central to Jewish life during this period? How does studying God's word help sustain faith during seasons when God feels quiet?

3. **Malachi confronted the people for offering God their leftovers instead of their best.** What are some ways people today might give God their "leftovers" in time, attention, or effort?

4. **God worked through the rise and fall of empires, the spread of a language, and the building of roads to prepare for Jesus.** What does this tell you about how God uses even secular events and unbelieving people to accomplish his purposes?

5. **The Jewish people waited four hundred years between Malachi and the coming of Jesus.** What do you think that kind of long, generational waiting does to a community's faith? What can we learn from the fact that messianic hope actually grew stronger, not weaker, during the wait?

The prophets have spoken their last words. The promises of God are hanging in the air, waiting to be fulfilled. The tiny community of Jewish people huddled behind Nehemiah's walls doesn't know it yet, but the world is about to change in ways none of them could imagine. A young Greek prince is sharpening his sword on the other side of the Mediterranean, and when he's finished, the world will never be the same.

Turn the page.

2

THE WORLD TURNS GREEK

Have you ever moved to a new school? Everything is different. The hallways don't make sense yet. The lunchroom has unwritten rules about where you sit and who you sit with. People use slang you've never heard. They dress differently, laugh at different things, care about different stuff. The teachers run their classrooms in ways you're not used to. And the pressure to fit in starts on day one. You don't want to stick out. You don't want to be the weird kid who does things the old way.

But here's the thing: if you change too much, you lose yourself. You start doing things you never would have done before, just because everyone else is doing them. Your old friends wouldn't recognize you. Your family wouldn't recognize you. And somewhere in the middle of all that adapting, you have to figure out a hard question: How much of the new world do I accept, and how much of who I am do I hold onto?

That's almost exactly what happened to the Jewish people about three hundred years before Jesus was born. They didn't move to a new school. The new school came to them. A young conqueror from a small kingdom in northern Greece swept across the known world in barely a decade, and when the dust settled, everything had changed. The language was different. The culture was different. The rules were different. And for the Jewish people, the pressure to fit in would become the defining struggle of the next two centuries.

His name was Alexander. And the world he created would never go back to the way it was before.

THE PRINCE WHO CONQUERED THE WORLD

Alexander III of Macedon wasn't supposed to be anyone special. Macedonia was the backwoods of the Greek world, a rough, rural kingdom that other Greeks looked down on. The great Athenian politician Demosthenes once dismissed Macedonia as a place where you couldn't even buy decent slaves.

But Alexander's father, Philip II, had bigger plans. Philip was a military genius who transformed the Macedonian army into the most disciplined fighting force in the ancient world. He united the constantly feuding Greek city-states under his control, something no one had ever managed before. And he hired no less a teacher than Aristotle, one of the greatest minds in human history, to tutor his son.

Then, in 336 BC, Philip was assassinated at a wedding celebration. Alexander was twenty years old. He inherited his father's army, his father's ambitions, and a plan to invade the mighty Persian Empire, the same empire that had ruled over the Jewish people for two centuries.

What happened next still astonishes historians.

In barely more than a decade, Alexander conquered virtually the entire known world. He defeated the Persian army at the Battle of Issus, then again at Gaugamela, where the Persian king Darius III fled the field and was later murdered by his own men. Alexander took Babylon, the richest city on earth. He seized the Persian capitals and their staggering treasuries of gold and silver. He pushed his army east through lands that are now Iran, Afghanistan, Pakistan, and India, crossing deserts and mountain ranges that seemed impossible to pass.

He founded cities everywhere he went. The most famous, Alexandria in Egypt, would become one of the greatest cities in the ancient world, a center of learning, culture, and trade that would shine for centuries. He named it after himself. Most of his cities, he named after himself.

Alexander never lost a battle. He was fearless in combat, leading charges personally, taking wounds that would have killed lesser men. His soldiers worshiped him. His enemies feared him. By the time he was twenty-five, a Babylonian scribe marked the change by dating a tablet to the reign of Alexander, "King of the World."

And then, at thirty-two, he died. A fever took him in Babylon in June of 323 BC, and just like that, the man who had conquered the world was gone.

AN EMPIRE IN PIECES

Alexander's death threw his empire into chaos. He left behind no clear heir. His generals, ambitious men who had fought beside him for years, immediately began scheming for control. They attempted to maintain the fiction of a united empire by ruling as regents for Alexander's infant son and his mentally impaired half-brother. But the fiction didn't last long.

Within two decades, the empire had splintered into rival kingdoms ruled by Alexander's former generals. Three dynasties emerged as the most powerful. Ptolemy took Egypt and made Alexandria his capital. Seleucus claimed the vast eastern territories, including Syria, Mesopotamia, and Persia. Antigonus and his descendants fought for control of Macedonia and Greece.

The Jewish homeland sat right in the middle, squeezed between the Ptolemaic kingdom in Egypt to the south and the Seleucid kingdom in Syria to the north. For the next century and a half, these two powers would fight over the small strip of land where God's people lived. The Jewish community became a prize to be traded, fought over, and taxed by whichever empire happened to hold them at the moment.

Alexander's empire was gone. But something far more lasting survived him.

THE GREEK TSUNAMI

Alexander didn't just conquer territories. He changed them. Everywhere his armies went, Greek culture followed. And unlike military conquest, which can be reversed when the soldiers go home, cultural conquest sinks roots that go deep and last for centuries.

This process has a name: Hellenization, from the Greek word for Greece. It was a tidal wave of cultural change that reshaped the ancient world.

Start with language. Before Alexander, the peoples of the ancient Near East spoke dozens of different languages. Communication between regions was difficult. But Alexander and his successors spread Greek everywhere. Within a few generations, Greek became the common language of trade, government, education, and literature across the entire Mediterranean world. A merchant in Egypt could do business with a trader in Syria, and they'd both speak Greek. A scholar in Jerusalem could read a philosopher in Athens, because they wrote in the same language.

This is why the New Testament was written in Greek. Not because Jesus spoke Greek (he probably spoke Aramaic), but because by the time his followers carried the gospel across the Roman Empire, Greek was the language everyone understood. God, in his providence, had spent centuries preparing a common language for the message of his Son.

Then came the culture. Greek cities were built on a pattern: a central marketplace, a gymnasium for athletic training and education, a theater for plays, a stadium for competitions. These weren't just buildings. They were an entire way of life. The gymnasium in particular was the heart of Greek culture. Young men trained there, studied there, formed friendships there. To be educated at a gymnasium was to be civilized. To reject the gymnasium was to be a barbarian.

Greek philosophy changed how people thought. Questions about the meaning of life, the nature of the soul, the existence of God, and the possibility of life after death entered conversations that had never included them before. Greek ideas about individual worth, about the importance of reason, about ethics and virtue spread alongside Greek language and architecture. Some of these ideas lined up surprisingly well with Jewish beliefs. Others collided with them head-on.

And Greek economics reshaped daily life. Alexander established a single currency based on a common standard. Trade routes expanded. The economy became more interconnected than ever before. Wealth flowed toward the new Greek cities, especially Alexandria, which became the economic engine of the Mediterranean world.

Within a generation or two, the entire eastern Mediterranean had been transformed. You could travel from Greece to Egypt to Persia and find Greek theaters, Greek schools, Greek coins, and Greek-speaking people everywhere you went.

A GREEK WORLD MEETS A JEWISH FAITH

For the Jewish people, this cultural tsunami posed a question that had never been so urgent before: How do we stay faithful to God in a world that wants us to become something else?

Under Persian rule, the pressure had been manageable. The Persians were generally tolerant. They let conquered peoples keep their customs, worship their gods, and live by their own laws. As long as you paid your taxes and didn't rebel, the Persians mostly left you alone.

The Greeks were different. Not because they were cruel (at least not at first) but because their culture was attractive. Greek education was sophisticated. Greek art was beautiful. Greek philosophy was intellectually exciting. Greek cities offered opportunity, wealth, and social advancement. If you wanted to get ahead in the new world Alexander had created, you needed to speak Greek, think Greek, and live Greek.

For some Jews, this was welcome. They saw no reason to be isolated from the wider world. They learned Greek, adopted Greek customs, and sent their sons to Greek schools. Some went further, wearing Greek clothing, taking Greek names, and participating in Greek athletic competitions. A few even tried to surgically reverse their circumcision so they wouldn't stand out at the gymnasium, where athletes trained naked.

For others, this was a nightmare. The law of Moses set the Jewish people apart from every other nation. Circumcision, dietary laws, Sabbath observance, the worship of one God alone—these weren't optional customs you could drop when they became inconvenient. They were the covenant identity of God's people. To abandon them was to abandon God himself. From this perspective, every Greek gymnasium was a threat. Every Greek philosophy was a potential idol. Every compromise was a step toward disappearing into the surrounding culture and losing everything that made Israel Israel.

This tension didn't explode immediately. For several generations, it simmered. Many Jews found a middle ground, using Greek language and even some Greek ways of thinking while holding firmly to the core of their faith. The Old Testament was translated into Greek in Alexandria, producing what we call the Septuagint, so that Greek-speaking Jews could still read the word of God. Jewish thinkers began using Greek categories to explain and defend their ancient beliefs.

But the middle ground was getting narrower. And in the next chapter, the pressure would begin to build toward a crisis that would force every Jewish person to choose a side.

WHAT THIS MEANS FOR US

First, culture is powerful, and it doesn't announce itself. The Jewish people didn't wake up one morning and decide to become Greek. It happened gradually: a new word here, a new custom there, a small compromise that seemed harmless at the time. That's how culture works on all of us. The values, habits, and assumptions of the world around you seep in slowly, and before you know it, you're thinking and living differently than you used to. Recognizing that process is the first step toward making conscious choices about what you accept and what you resist.

Second, faithfulness sometimes means being different. The Jewish people were called to be set apart. That wasn't always comfortable, especially when the surrounding culture offered real benefits. Being different can feel lonely, awkward, and costly. But God didn't call his people to blend in. He called them to stand out, not to be arrogant, but to be distinct. If your faith never puts you at odds with the culture around you, it's worth asking whether you're following God or just following the crowd.

Third, God can use anything for his purposes. Greek culture was the product of human ambition and military conquest. But God used it anyway. He used the Greek language to prepare the way for the gospel. He used Greek roads and trade routes to connect the world. He used Greek philosophical questions to create an audience hungry for answers that only the truth of Scripture could provide. God is not limited to working through godly people. He can take the ambitions of a pagan conqueror and weave them into his plan for the salvation of the world.

Fourth, knowing who you are protects you from becoming someone else. The Jews who held onto their faith during Hellenization didn't do it by accident. They did it by knowing their Scriptures, practicing their worship, and reminding themselves daily who they belonged to. Identity isn't passive.

It has to be built, practiced, and defended. The same is true for you. If you don't know what you believe and why you believe it, you'll eventually believe whatever the loudest voice around you is saying.

TALKING POINTS

1. **Alexander conquered the known world by the time he was thirty. His empire collapsed almost immediately after his death, but Greek culture lasted for centuries.** Why do you think cultural influence is often more lasting than military power?

2. **Some Jews embraced Greek culture while others resisted it fiercely.** If you had been a Jewish teenager during this period, which side do you think you would have been drawn to, and why?

3. **The Old Testament was translated into Greek so that people outside of Israel could read them.** How do you think this affected the spread of God's word? What does it tell us about God's willingness to meet people where they are?

4. **Greek culture offered real benefits: education, economic opportunity, sophisticated art and philosophy.** What are some things in your own culture that are genuinely good but that might still pull you away from faithfulness to God if you're not careful?

5. **The tension between adopting the surrounding culture and holding onto your faith is something every generation of believers has faced.** What are the pressures you feel today to "fit in" with the world around you, and how do you decide where to draw the line?

Alexander's empire is gone, but his legacy is everywhere. Greek is the language of power, Greek cities dot the landscape, and Greek ideas are reshaping how people think about everything from God to government. The Jewish people are learning to navigate this new world, some with enthusiasm and some with deep unease. But for now, the pressure is manageable. The Greek rulers are mostly tolerant. The temple still stands. The faith survives.

That's about to change. Two rival empires are circling the Jewish homeland like wolves, and the Jewish community is about to find itself caught between them, with no way out.

Turn the page.

3

CAUGHT BETWEEN EMPIRES

The 1998 film *The Parent Trap* tells the story of twin sisters, Hallie and Annie, who were separated as babies when their parents divorced. One grew up in California with their dad. The other grew up in London with their mom. Neither twin knew the other existed until they accidentally met at summer camp.

But here's the part of the movie that sticks with you: neither girl chose the divorce. Neither one asked to be separated from her sister. Their lives were shaped entirely by a conflict between two powerful adults they couldn't control. They didn't get a vote. They didn't get a say. They just had to live with the consequences and figure out how to survive in a situation someone else created.

For about a hundred and fifty years, that's almost exactly what happened to the Jewish people. After Alexander the Great died and his empire shattered into rival kingdoms, the Jewish homeland ended up stuck between two of the largest pieces: the Ptolemaic kingdom in Egypt and the Seleucid kingdom in Syria. These two empires spent generations fighting over the tiny strip of land where God's people lived. The Jews didn't start the fight. They didn't choose sides. They were just there, caught in the middle, while armies marched back and forth across their farms, their villages, and their sacred city.

And like the twins in the movie, they had to figure out how to hold onto who they were while the world around them kept shifting.

THE TUG-OF-WAR BEGINS

When Alexander's empire fell apart, his generals carved it into rival kingdoms. Two of them matter most for our story.

Ptolemy, one of Alexander's most trusted companions, took control of Egypt. He was shrewd, patient, and ambitious. He made Alexandria his capital, and under his leadership it became one of the greatest cities the ancient world had ever seen. His dynasty, the Ptolemies, would rule Egypt for nearly three centuries.

Seleucus, another general, claimed the vast eastern territories, including Syria, Mesopotamia, and Persia. His dynasty, the Seleucids, built their capital at Antioch in Syria. They controlled an enormous kingdom stretching from the Mediterranean to the borders of India.

And right between these two empires, like a fence between two feuding neighbors, sat the land of Israel.

Both empires wanted it. The land sat on a crucial trade route connecting Africa, Asia, and the Mediterranean coast. Whoever held it controlled a strategic gateway. So the Ptolemies and Seleucids fought over it. Not once or twice, but repeatedly, across multiple wars spanning more than a century.

In the fifty years leading up to the decisive Battle of Ipsus in 301 BC, control of the Jewish homeland changed hands at least nine times. Nine times in fifty years. Imagine living in a country where the government changes every five or six years, not by election but by invasion. Armies march through your fields. Foreign soldiers camp in your city. Your taxes go to a different king every few years. You never know who's in charge next, but you know one thing for certain: it won't be you.

LIFE UNDER THE PTOLEMIES

After 301 BC, the Ptolemies won the tug-of-war and held onto the Jewish homeland for about a century. This period wasn't as traumatic as the decades that came before, but it was far from easy.

The Ptolemies ran their kingdom like a business, and the business existed to make the king rich. The entire economy was designed to funnel wealth toward Alexandria. Ptolemy II introduced a cash economy, dramatically increasing the minting of coins. This made trade more efficient, but it also made taxation more aggressive. The average person was taxed multiple times, in multiple ways, and the system was ruthless.

The Ptolemies didn't collect taxes directly. They sold the right to collect taxes to private contractors called tax farmers. These men paid the king an agreed amount up front, then went out and collected as much as they could from the population. Everything they collected above the agreed amount was their profit. The more aggressively they squeezed people, the richer they got.

It was legalized extortion. Tax farmers used intimidation, threats, and brute force to extract money from ordinary families.

People who couldn't pay lost their land, fell into debt slavery, or were forced into desperate measures just to survive. The system bred resentment that burned for generations. When Jesus walked into the life of a tax collector named Matthew centuries later and said "Follow me," he was reaching into one of the most hated professions in the Jewish world. That hatred didn't start in the first century. It started here, under the Ptolemies.

Meanwhile, the Jewish community in Egypt was growing rapidly. Ptolemy had conscripted Jewish soldiers and relocated Jewish families to Alexandria after conquering Jerusalem. Over time, the Jewish population in Egypt became large and influential. Alexandria became the most important center of Jewish life outside of Jerusalem.

These Egyptian Jews spoke Greek. Many of them had never spoken anything else. And that created a problem: they couldn't read their own Scriptures, which were written in Hebrew.

THE BIBLE IN GREEK

The solution was one of the most important events in all of religious history, though almost nobody noticed it at the time.

Sometime during the third century BC, Jewish scholars in Alexandria began translating the Hebrew Scriptures into Greek. The project started with the five books of Moses and eventually expanded to include the rest of the Old Testament. The result is called the Septuagint.

This matters far more than it might seem. For the first time, the word of God was available in the common language of the Mediterranean world. A Greek-speaking Jew in Alexandria could now read the law of Moses. A curious Greek merchant could pick up a copy and encounter the God of Israel. When the early Christians carried the gospel across the Roman Empire generations later, the Bible they carried was the Septuagint. When the apostle Paul quoted Scripture in his letters, he usually quoted from this Greek translation.

God wasn't sending prophets during this period. But through the quiet work of scholars with ink and parchment, he was making sure his word would be ready when the time came. The Septuagint was providence disguised as a translation project.

THE SELEUCIDS TAKE OVER

Around 200 BC, the balance of power shifted. The Seleucid king Antiochus III, known as "Antiochus the Great," finally wrested the Jewish homeland away from the Ptolemies after a decisive military victory. The Jews, tired of Ptolemaic taxation, welcomed the change. Antiochus seemed like an improvement. He granted the Jews significant freedoms: the right to live according to their ancestral laws, tax relief for the city of Jerusalem, and funding to repair the temple.

For a brief moment, things looked promising. Under early Seleucid rule, Jerusalem grew into a significant urban center for the first time in centuries. Construction projects expanded the city. Wealth flowed in. The temple was refurbished. The Jewish community had more political breathing room than it had enjoyed in a long time.

But the honeymoon didn't last.

Antiochus III overreached. He pushed his empire westward into Greece and ran headlong into a rising power that would eventually swallow the entire Mediterranean world: Rome. In 190 BC, the Romans crushed his army at the Battle of Magnesia and imposed devastating terms. Antiochus was forced to surrender vast territories, hand over hostages (including his own son), and pay an enormous sum in war reparations.

The financial pressure was suffocating. To pay Rome, the Seleucids needed revenue. That meant squeezing their subjects harder. The generous concessions Antiochus had given the Jews suddenly became less secure. The economic screws began to tighten. And the political landscape grew more unstable with each passing year.

A PEOPLE PULLING APART

Underneath the politics, a deeper crisis was building inside the Jewish community. The question that had been simmering since Alexander's conquest was now reaching a boil: How Greek should the Jewish people become?

On one side were the Hellenizers, mostly from wealthy and aristocratic families. They saw Greek culture as the path to prosperity and influence. They wanted Jerusalem to become a fully Greek city, complete with a gymnasium, a Greek-style government, and full participation in the cultural life of the Hellenistic world. Some of them held positions of power, including influence over the high priesthood itself.

On the other side were the traditionalists. They believed that the law of Moses was the foundation of Jewish identity and that compromising with Greek culture was a betrayal of the covenant. For them, every step toward Hellenization was a step away from God.

The tension wasn't just theoretical. It played out in real conflicts over real issues. Should Jewish young men train naked at a Greek gymnasium? Should Jewish leaders adopt Greek names and wear Greek clothing? Should the high priesthood be something a man could buy from a foreign king by offering the highest bribe?

That last question wasn't hypothetical. In 174 BC, a man named Jason offered the Seleucid king Antiochus IV a large sum of money in exchange for being appointed high priest, replacing his own brother. The king agreed. Just like that, the most sacred office in Jewish religion was sold to the highest bidder. Jason then began transforming Jerusalem into a Greek city. He built a gymnasium. He changed the city's constitution. He encouraged young priests to abandon their duties and spend their time at athletic competitions instead.

The traditionalists were horrified. And it was about to get worse.

Within a few years, another man named Menelaus outbid Jason for the high priesthood with an even larger bribe. Menelaus wasn't even from the traditional priestly family. The office that God had established through Moses, the role that connected the entire nation to the presence of God, was now controlled by the man willing to pay the most for it.

The community was tearing itself apart. The culture war between Hellenizers and traditionalists was escalating toward violence. And the Seleucid king who held the power to settle the dispute was about to make a decision that would push the entire Jewish nation to the breaking point.

WHAT THIS MEANS FOR US

First, faithfulness gets harder when the pressure comes from inside. The Jewish people could handle foreign armies. What nearly destroyed them was the division within their own community. When people who claim to follow God can't agree on what faithfulness looks like, the result is often more damaging than anything an outside enemy could do. Be careful about how you handle disagreements within your own church and community. Division from within is one of the most dangerous forces in the world.

Second, money corrupts what it touches. The high priesthood was supposed to be sacred. It was supposed to be about serving God and representing the people. But when it became something you could buy, it lost its integrity. The same thing happens today whenever someone uses faith as a tool for personal gain, whether that's money, power, or influence. Guard the things that are supposed to be sacred. Don't let them become transactions.

Third, God's word will find a way to reach people. The Septuagint was born out of necessity. Greek-speaking Jews needed the Scriptures in their language. But God used that necessity to prepare the way for something far bigger than anyone at the time could have imagined. The gospel would one day travel across the Roman Empire in the very language those Alexandrian scholars chose for their translation. God's word is never trapped. It always finds a way to the people who need it.

Fourth, being caught in circumstances you didn't choose doesn't mean God has abandoned you. The Jewish people didn't ask to be squeezed between two empires. They didn't choose the wars, the taxes, or the cultural pressure. But God was with them through all of it, preserving them, shaping them, and preparing them for something they couldn't yet see. You may be living in circumstances you didn't choose right now. That doesn't mean you're outside of God's plan. It may mean you're right in the middle of it.

TALKING POINTS

1. **The Jewish homeland changed hands nine times in fifty years.** What do you think that kind of instability does to a community's sense of identity and security? How do you think it affected their trust in God?

2. **The Ptolemaic tax system created enormous suffering for ordinary people and bred deep hatred toward tax collectors.** Knowing this background, why do you think Jesus' willingness to eat with tax collectors and even call one as a disciple was so shocking?

3. **The Septuagint made God's word available to people who couldn't read Hebrew.** What are some ways God's word is being made accessible to new audiences today? Why does translation matter for the spread of the gospel?

4. **The high priesthood was sold to the highest bidder, turning a sacred office into a political tool.** What happens when spiritual leadership becomes more about power and money than about serving God? How can we protect spiritual leadership from that kind of corruption?

5. **The tension between Hellenizers and traditionalists forced every Jewish person to decide how much of the surrounding culture to accept.** What are some areas in your

own life where you feel pulled between your faith and the culture around you? How do you decide what to accept and what to resist?

42

The Jewish people are splitting down the middle. The wealthy and powerful are racing toward a Greek future. The devout are clinging to the law of Moses with everything they have. And a Seleucid king named Antiochus IV is watching it all from his throne, about to make a move that will pour gasoline on the fire.

The line in the sand is about to be drawn. And once it is, there will be no going back.

Turn the page.

4

THE LINE IN THE SAND

Sophocles, one of the greatest writers of ancient Greece, told a story called *Antigone* about a young woman who faced an impossible choice. Her brother had been killed in battle, and the king, Creon, issued a decree: no one was allowed to bury him. His body was to rot in the open as a public disgrace. Anyone who disobeyed would be executed.

For a Greek, leaving a body unburied was one of the worst things imaginable. It meant the soul would never find rest. Antigone believed that the gods required her to bury her brother, no matter what any human king said. So she did it. She broke the king's law to obey what she believed was a higher law.

When Creon found out, he was furious. He gave her a chance to back down. She refused. "I was not born to share in hate," she told him, "but in love." Creon sentenced her to death.

That story has haunted readers for over two thousand years because the question it asks never goes away: What do you do when a human authority commands you to violate what you believe God requires? Do you obey the king and survive? Or do you obey God and face the consequences?

In 167 BC, every Jewish person in Judea was forced to answer that question for real.

THE KING WHO CALLED HIMSELF GOD

To understand how things got so bad, you need to meet the man responsible. His name was Antiochus IV, and he was the king of the Seleucid Empire. He came to power in 175 BC, and from the start, he was a complicated figure.

Antiochus had spent years as a political hostage in Rome, watching how the Romans ran their empire. He admired their power and their culture. When he finally took the Seleucid throne, he was ambitious, theatrical, and deeply concerned with his own image. He gave himself the title "Epiphanes," which means "God Manifest." He wanted people to believe he was the visible expression of the divine on earth.

Not everyone bought it. Some of his subjects whispered a different nickname behind his back: "Epimanes," meaning "the Madman."

As we saw in the last chapter, the internal divisions among the Jewish people had already opened the door for trouble. The high priesthood had been sold to the highest bidder. First Jason bribed Antiochus for the position, then Menelaus outbid Jason with an even larger offer. The most sacred office in Judaism had become a commercial transaction, and the men holding it were more interested in Greek culture than in faithfully serving God.

But things were about to get incomparably worse.

THE SPARK

In 168 BC, Antiochus invaded Egypt for the second time. He was on the verge of conquering the entire country when something unexpected happened. A Roman ambassador named Gaius Popilius Laenas met him outside Alexandria, handed him a letter from the Roman Senate demanding he withdraw, and drew a circle in the sand around the king's feet. "Before you step out of that circle," the Roman told him, "give me an answer for the Senate."

Antiochus was humiliated. Rome was the one power he couldn't challenge. He withdrew from Egypt, seething with rage.

Back in Jerusalem, a rumor had spread that Antiochus was dead. Jason, the former high priest who had been replaced by Menelaus, used the moment to launch a coup, storming into the city with a small army to reclaim his position. It was Jew against Jew, fighting over an office that had already been corrupted.

When Antiochus learned what had happened, he took his fury out on Jerusalem. He sent his army under a commander named Apollonius, who arrived with promises of peace and then, on a Sabbath when the people were resting, unleashed a massacre. Thousands of Jews were killed. Houses were looted and burned. Women and children were enslaved. The city walls around the temple were torn down. A massive military fortress called the Acra was built to dominate the skyline, housing a permanent garrison of soldiers and Hellenizing Jews loyal to the king.

Conservative Jews who survived fled the city, some clutching scrolls of Scripture as they ran. Jerusalem, the holy city, was no longer theirs.

THE DECREE

Then Antiochus did something no foreign ruler had ever done to the Jewish people. He revoked their status as a distinct nation within his empire. Until now, the Jews had been recognized as an official ethnic group with the legal right to practice their ancestral customs. That right was gone.

The consequences were devastating. The Jewish religion was effectively outlawed. Everything that made the Jewish people distinctive was stripped away by royal decree.

The temple was rededicated to the Greek god Zeus. A pagan altar was erected on top of the altar of burnt offering. Pigs, the most unclean animal in Jewish law, were sacrificed on it. The book of Daniel calls this "the abomination of desolation" (Daniel 11:31), and it became one of the most traumatic images in all of Jewish memory.

Circumcision was banned. Any mother caught circumcising her son faced execution. In at least two recorded cases, women who defied the ban were paraded through the streets with their babies tied around their necks and then thrown from the city walls.

Sabbath observance was forbidden. The day that set the Jewish people apart, the day that reminded them every week that they belonged to God, was no longer legal.

Copies of the Scriptures were hunted down and destroyed. Possessing a scroll of the law became a capital offense.

Jews were forced to eat pork sacrificed to pagan gods. Participation in the king's birthday celebrations became a mandatory loyalty test. Refusal was treated as treason, punishable by death. A festival honoring the Greek god Dionysus was imposed, complete with public processions that violated every standard of Jewish decency.

The goal was not just political control. It was the erasure of Jewish identity. Antiochus wanted the Jewish people to disappear into the surrounding culture, to become Greeks in everything but ancestry, to worship his gods and call him divine. He wanted to dissolve the covenant people of God into the Hellenistic world as if they had never existed.

THOSE WHO REFUSED

Some Jews complied. Under the crushing weight of threats, torture, and death, many participated in the new rituals, ate the forbidden food, and hid whatever faith they still had deep inside where no one could see it. It is difficult to judge them. The pressure was unimaginable.

But others refused.

An elderly scribe named Eleazar, ninety years old, was ordered to eat pork from a pagan sacrifice. Friends offered to sneak him kosher meat so he could pretend to comply without actually breaking the law. Eleazar refused even the appearance of compromise. He said that pretending would mislead younger Jews into thinking he had abandoned his faith. He willingly submitted to torture and death rather than give anyone a reason to think God's law could be discarded when the cost of keeping it got too high.

A mother and her seven sons were brought before the king himself and ordered to eat sacrificial pork. One by one, each son refused. One by one, each was tortured and killed in front of the others and in front of their mother. The youngest son told the king directly that God would vindicate them and raise them to new life, while the king would face divine judgment. The mother watched all seven of her sons die and then died herself.

These stories were told and retold for generations. They became the foundation of a theology of martyrdom that would shape Jewish and Christian thinking for centuries. The conviction was simple and fierce: there are things worse than death. Losing your identity as one of God's people is one of them.

THE HAMMER FALLS

Not everyone chose the path of quiet martyrdom. Some decided to fight.

An old priest named Mattathias lived in the village of Modein, in the lowlands between Jerusalem and the coast. When the king's enforcers arrived to impose the royal cult, they singled out Mattathias as a prominent citizen and offered him a deal: be the first to sacrifice, and the king will make you a "friend of the king," with all the wealth and status that comes with it.

Mattathias refused. And when another man stepped forward to offer the sacrifice in his place, Mattathias snapped. He struck the man down, killed the royal official, and tore down the altar.

Then he ran.

His five sons ran with him. They fled into the Judean hills with a small group of followers and began something that nobody expected: an armed resistance against the most powerful empire in the eastern Mediterranean.

Mattathias likely died shortly after, but his sons carried on. The middle son, Judas, quickly emerged as the leader. He was fearless, cunning, and brutal. He earned the nickname "Maccabeus," meaning "the Hammer." His fighters were outnumbered, poorly armed, and operating from caves and hilltops. But they knew the terrain. They used ambushes and guerrilla tactics. And they were fighting for something the Seleucid soldiers were not: their identity, their faith, and their very existence as a people.

The Maccabean revolt had begun. And against all odds, the Hammer was about to strike.

WHAT THIS MEANS FOR US

First, there are lines that should never be crossed. Antiochus didn't just change the government. He tried to erase a people's identity and replace their God with a counterfeit. Some things are not negotiable, no matter what the cost. Knowing where your lines are before you're tested is one of the most important things you can do. Eleazar didn't decide in the moment. He had already decided long before the test arrived.

Second, faithfulness under pressure is never wasted. The martyrs of this period didn't live to see the outcome. They died without knowing whether their stand would make any difference. But their example inspired an entire nation and shaped the faith of generations that followed. You may never see the results of your faithfulness. That doesn't mean it's wasted. Someone is always watching, and your courage may be the thing that gives them courage.

Third, the people who look weakest are sometimes the strongest. An elderly scribe. A mother with her children. A village priest in a backwater town. None of them looked like they could challenge an empire. But their refusal to bend did more to preserve the faith than any army could have done. God has always worked through people the world overlooks.

Fourth, identity must be actively defended. Antiochus understood something powerful: if you can change what people believe about themselves, you can change everything. The Jewish people survived because enough of them refused to let go of who they were, even when holding on cost them everything. Your identity as a follower of God isn't something that just happens. It's something you choose, defend, and hold onto, especially when the world is telling you to let it go.

TALKING POINTS

1. **Antiochus tried to erase Jewish identity by outlawing circumcision, Sabbath, and the Scriptures.** Why do you think he targeted those specific practices? What do those practices represent about the relationship between God and his people?

2. **Eleazar refused even to pretend to comply with the king's orders, saying it would mislead younger people.** Do you think he was right? Why does the appearance of compromise matter, not just the reality of it?

3. **The mother who watched her seven sons die rather than abandon the faith is one of the most powerful stories from this period.** What do you think gave her and her sons that kind of courage? Could you imagine having that kind of conviction?

4. **Mattathias responded to the crisis with violence. The martyrs responded with quiet endurance. Both responses came from a deep commitment to God.** Do you think one response was more faithful than the other? Why or why not?

5. **Antiochus understood that if you change what people believe about themselves, you can reshape an entire culture.** What are some ways the culture around you tries to redefine who you are or what you should value? How do you resist that pressure?

A priest and his sons are hiding in the hills with a handful of fighters, armed with stolen weapons and burning conviction. The most powerful empire in the eastern Mediterranean is about to send its armies to crush them. By every reasonable calculation, the Maccabees should be wiped out in a matter of weeks.

They won't be.

Turn the page.

5

HAMMERS, HEROES, AND TYRANTS

The Goonies is one of those movies that never gets old. A group of kids from a small town discover an old treasure map and decide to follow it, hoping the pirate gold at the end will save their families from losing their homes. They're up against everything: booby traps, underground caves, a family of criminals chasing them, and the simple fact that they're just kids with no business being on this kind of adventure.

But they don't quit. Every time the situation looks hopeless, somebody figures something out. They argue. They get scared. They almost give up more than once. And then, against every reasonable expectation, they find the treasure. The kids who nobody took seriously pull off something impossible.

There's a moment near the end when one of them says, "Goonies never say die." That line works because they've earned it. They didn't just stumble into victory. They fought for it, step by step, with nothing but courage, cleverness, and the stubborn refusal to surrender.

The Maccabees would have understood.

In 164 BC, a ragtag band of Jewish fighters pulled off one of the most improbable victories in ancient history. They were outmanned, outarmed, and facing a professional military that had crushed larger rebellions without breaking a sweat. They had no business winning. But they didn't quit either. And what they accomplished changed the course of Jewish history.

What came after, though, is a more complicated story.

THE HAMMER STRIKES

After the events at Modein, the Hasmonean brothers and their growing band of followers operated as guerrilla fighters in the Judean hills. Judas Maccabeus, the Hammer, proved to be a military leader of extraordinary ability. He understood that his small force could never defeat the Seleucid army in open combat. So he didn't try. He used the terrain, launched surprise attacks, and picked his battles with devastating precision.

The Seleucid authorities sent a governor named Apollonius with a police force to hunt the rebels down. Judas ambushed him, killed him personally, and took his sword as a trophy. A larger force under a commander named Seron came next. Judas caught his soldiers climbing a steep mountain pass and routed them before they could form ranks. Each victory brought more fighters to the cause and made the Maccabees impossible to ignore.

The Seleucid regent, Lysias, took personal command. He tried to outflank the rebels by approaching from the south, bringing a massive force to the border fortress at Beth Zur. The situation looked hopeless for the Maccabees. They were outnumbered, outpositioned, and running out of room to maneuver.

Then something completely unexpected happened. In late November of 164 BC, word arrived that Antiochus IV had died suddenly while campaigning in Persia. Lysias immediately abandoned his offensive and raced back to the capital to secure the succession. The crushing weight that had been bearing down on the Maccabees simply vanished.

The rebels couldn't believe it. From their perspective, God had intervened at the last possible moment. The tyrant was dead. The army had withdrawn. Against all odds, they were still standing.

THE TEMPLE RESTORED

With Lysias gone, the Maccabees seized their chance. They marched on Jerusalem, took control of the temple mount, and found the sanctuary in ruins. The pagan altar was still standing where it had been erected three years earlier. Idols littered the grounds. The sacred vessels were gone or defiled. Weeds grew in the courtyards.

The scene was heartbreaking, but also galvanizing. The fighters who had been killing and dying for this moment now set aside their weapons and became builders. They tore down the defiled altar and built a new one from uncut stones, following the instructions of the law of Moses. They crafted new sacred vessels, lit fresh lamps, and burned incense for the first time in years. They cleansed the courts and restored the building as closely as they could to what it had been.

On the twenty-fifth day of the month of Kislev, in December 164 BC, exactly three years after Antiochus had desecrated the temple, the Maccabees rededicated it. There was music, singing, celebration, and sacrifice. The joy was overwhelming. They decreed that the anniversary would be celebrated every year for eight days.

That festival is still celebrated today. It's called Hanukkah, which means "dedication." Every year, Jewish families light candles for eight nights in memory of the day their ancestors took back their temple from the forces that tried to destroy their faith.

VICTORY AND LOSS

But the war wasn't over. The Seleucids still controlled the massive fortress called the Acra in the heart of Jerusalem. Hellenizing Jews still had power in certain areas. And the surrounding nations, many of them hostile to the Jewish revival, launched attacks on Jewish communities throughout the region.

Judas fought on. He conducted campaigns to rescue besieged Jewish communities in Galilee and across the Jordan River. He defeated Seleucid forces multiple times. His reputation grew until he was known throughout the region as one of the most capable military leaders of his generation.

But the Seleucids kept coming back. In 160 BC, a large Seleucid army marched into Judea under the command of a general named Bacchides. Many of Judas' fighters deserted when they saw the size of the force. Only eight hundred stayed with him.

Judas fought anyway. He charged the Seleucid right flank and pushed it back, but the left closed in behind him. Surrounded and outnumbered, Judas Maccabeus fell in battle. The Hammer was dead.

It should have been the end of the movement. But Judas had brothers.

FROM REBELS TO RULERS

Jonathan, the youngest and cleverest of the Hasmonean brothers, took over the cause and transformed it. Where Judas had been a warrior, Jonathan was a politician. He played rival claimants to the Seleucid throne against each other, offering his support to whichever contender would give the Jews the most concessions. Through this shrewd maneuvering, he gained control of the high priesthood, making himself both the military leader of the Jewish resistance and the religious leader of the nation.

When Jonathan was captured and killed through treachery in 143 BC, the last surviving brother, Simon, took command. Simon was the strategist who had been working behind the scenes for years. In 142 BC, he achieved what none of his brothers had lived to see: full independence. The Seleucids formally recognized Judea as a free state. Simon expelled the Seleucid garrison from the Acra. For the first time in over four centuries, since the Babylonian conquest in 586 BC, the Jewish people governed themselves.

Simon was declared leader of the nation with the combined titles of high priest, military commander, and civil governor. The people enshrined this arrangement in an official decree, with one important condition: his authority would remain in effect "until a trustworthy prophet should arise." Even in their moment of triumph, the Jewish people recognized that the Hasmonean settlement might not be God's final arrangement for the nation. They left room for God to redirect things in the future.

BECOMING WHAT THEY FOUGHT AGAINST

Under Simon and his successors, the Hasmonean dynasty ruled an independent Jewish kingdom for about eighty years. And this is where the story turns tragic.

Simon's son, John Hyrcanus, expanded the kingdom dramatically, conquering Samaria and destroying the Samaritan temple on Mount Gerizim. He also conquered the region of Idumea to the south and forced its inhabitants to convert to Judaism. His military successes made the Hasmonean kingdom larger than it had been since the days of Solomon.

But expansion came at a cost. John Hyrcanus fell out with the Pharisees, who had been early supporters of the Maccabean cause. He aligned himself instead with the Sadducees, the wealthy priestly aristocracy. The movement that had started as a populist rebellion was becoming an establishment dynasty.

Things got worse under his successors. His son Aristobulus took the title "king," something no Hasmonean had done before. He imprisoned his own mother, letting her starve to death, and murdered his brother. The next ruler, Alexander Jannaeus, was even more brutal. He waged wars of conquest, crucified hundreds of his own people during a civil conflict, and combined the offices of king and high priest so thoroughly that the original purposes of both were lost.

The irony was devastating. The Maccabees had fought to preserve Jewish identity against a foreign tyrant. Now their descendants had become tyrants themselves, behaving like the

Greek kings their ancestors had died resisting. They waged the same kind of wars, played the same political games, and oppressed the same common people. The revolution that had started with an old priest refusing to bow had produced a dynasty that bowed to nothing but its own ambition.

By the time the Hasmonean dynasty collapsed into a vicious civil war between two brothers fighting over the throne, the Jewish people were exhausted, disillusioned, and desperate for something better.

And Rome was watching.

WHAT THIS MEANS FOR US

First, God can use imperfect people to accomplish extraordinary things. The Maccabees were violent, sometimes brutal, and far from perfect. But God used their courage and determination to preserve the Jewish people and their faith at a moment when both were on the verge of extinction. God doesn't wait for perfect instruments. He uses the ones who show up.

Second, winning isn't the same as finishing. The Maccabees won an astonishing military victory. But victory on the battlefield didn't solve the deeper problems of the heart. Power corrupted the dynasty that followed, proving that external victory without internal transformation always falls short. The same is true in your own life. Winning an argument, getting what you want, or defeating an opponent doesn't mean the real work is done.

Third, every human institution eventually disappoints. The Hasmonean dynasty started with heroism and ended with fratricide. The people who saved the nation became the people who abused it. This is a pattern that repeats throughout history: human institutions, no matter how nobly they begin, eventually bend under the weight of human sin. Only God's kingdom doesn't decay.

Fourth, the door was left open for God to act. Even at the height of Hasmonean power, the people acknowledged that a trustworthy prophet might still arise. They knew this wasn't the final chapter. That instinct was right. God was not finished. The best was still to come.

TALKING POINTS

1. **The Maccabees started as a small group with makeshift weapons and defeated a professional army.** What does their story teach you about what God can do through people who refuse to give up, even when the odds are against them?

2. **The rededication of the temple (Hanukkah) is still celebrated today, over two thousand years later.** Why do you think this moment mattered so much to the Jewish people? What does it mean to rededicate something to God after it's been lost or defiled?

3. **The Hasmonean dynasty started with heroes and ended with tyrants.** How does power change people? What safeguards can prevent leaders from becoming the very thing they originally opposed?

4. **The decree establishing the Hasmonean dynasty included the condition "until a trustworthy prophet should arise."** Why do you think the people included that condition? What does it tell us about their understanding of God's ongoing purposes?

5. The Maccabean story raises hard questions about violence and faithfulness. Was the Maccabees' decision to fight the right one? Are there situations where violence is justified in defense of faith, or should believers always choose nonviolent resistance? What did Jesus teach about this?

The Hasmonean kingdom is tearing itself apart. Two brothers are fighting over a throne that neither of them deserves. The nation that clawed its way to independence through blood and courage is about to lose everything it gained. And from the west, a power greater than anything the Jewish people have ever faced is stretching its shadow across the Mediterranean.

The eagle is about to land.

Turn the page.

6

THE EAGLE LANDS

Nearly five hundred years ago, an Italian political thinker named Niccolo Machiavelli wrote a book called *The Prince*. It was a handbook for rulers, and it was ice cold. Machiavelli didn't waste time talking about how leaders *should* behave in an ideal world. He was interested in how they actually behave in the real one.

His advice was blunt. A new ruler who takes power must eliminate anyone who might challenge him. He should appear religious without actually being controlled by religion. He should be generous when it costs him nothing and ruthless when his throne is at stake. And if he must choose between being loved and being feared, he should choose fear every time, because love depends on the goodwill of others, but fear depends only on the ruler himself.

The Prince shocked readers when it was published. It still does. But if Machiavelli had lived about fifteen hundred years earlier and traveled to Judea, he would have found a king who followed his playbook almost perfectly, centuries before it was written.

His name was Herod. And his rise to power is one of the most ruthless stories in the ancient world.

ROME ARRIVES

Before Herod, there was Rome. And Rome didn't tiptoe into the story. By the middle of the first century BC, the Roman Republic had become the most powerful force on earth. Roman armies had already conquered Greece, crushed Carthage, and pushed into Asia Minor. Now the Roman general Pompey was sweeping through the eastern Mediterranean, absorbing territories and redrawing the map.

When he arrived in the region in 63 BC, the Hasmonean kingdom was in the middle of a civil war. Two brothers, Hyrcanus II and Aristobulus II, were fighting each other for the throne. Both of them appealed to Pompey for support, each hoping Rome would tip the scales in his favor.

It was a catastrophic miscalculation. When you invite a wolf into your house to settle a family argument, don't be surprised when the wolf decides to stay.

Pompey sided with Hyrcanus, the weaker brother, precisely because a weak ruler would be easier to control. When Aristobulus' supporters barricaded themselves inside the temple, Pompey laid siege to it. His soldiers breached the walls on a Sabbath, knowing the defenders would be reluctant to fight. Hundreds of priests and defenders were slaughtered. Then Pompey did something that sent shockwaves through the Jewish world: he walked into the holy of holies, the innermost room of the temple where only the high priest was allowed to enter once a year.

He didn't plunder the temple. He didn't tear it down. He just looked inside, satisfying his own curiosity. But the violation was profound. A pagan general had walked into the most sacred space on earth, the place where God's presence was understood to dwell, and treated it like a tourist attraction.

Jewish independence was over. The kingdom the Maccabees had fought and died for, the freedom that had lasted barely eighty years, was gone. Judea became a Roman client state, stripped of its conquered territories, forced to pay tribute, and subject to the oversight of the Roman governor of Syria.

THE RISE OF HEROD

In the chaos that followed Rome's takeover, one family rose above all others: the family of Antipater, an Idumean politician who had been pulling strings behind the Hasmonean throne for years. Antipater was not Jewish by ancestry. His family came from Idumea, the region south of Judea whose inhabitants had been forcibly converted to Judaism by the Hasmonean king John Hyrcanus. But Antipater understood power better than any of the Hasmonean princes, and he understood one thing above all else: the future belonged to whoever had Rome's favor.

Antipater positioned himself as Rome's most reliable ally in the region. He supported Pompey, then switched his loyalty to Julius Caesar when Pompey fell. When Caesar needed military help during a crisis in Egypt, Antipater provided it. Caesar rewarded him by making him the effective ruler of Judea, with the weak Hyrcanus II serving as a figurehead high priest.

Antipater groomed his sons for power. His second son, Herod, was appointed governor of Galilee at the age of twenty-five. Herod proved himself immediately, crushing a rebel warlord with such efficiency that even the Roman governor of Syria took notice.

When Antipater was poisoned in 43 BC, Herod was ready. Through a combination of military skill, political cunning, and sheer audacity, he navigated the Roman civil wars that followed the assassination of Julius Caesar. He backed Mark Antony. He traveled to Rome itself and personally appealed to the Roman Senate. In 40 BC, the Senate did something extraordinary: they declared Herod "King of the Jews."

There was just one problem. He didn't actually control Judea yet. The last Hasmonean king, Mattathias Antigonus, was still on the throne, backed by the Parthian Empire from the east. It took Herod three years of brutal campaigning, with Roman military support, to conquer his own kingdom. In 37 BC, he finally took Jerusalem after a bloody siege.

The Hasmonean dynasty was finished. Herod was king.

THE BUILDER AND THE MONSTER

Herod the Great, as he came to be known, was one of the most complex figures in ancient history. He was simultaneously one of the greatest builders the ancient world had ever seen and one of the most paranoid, violent rulers who ever lived.

His building projects were staggering. He constructed entire cities from the ground up, including Caesarea on the Mediterranean coast, complete with a massive artificial harbor, temples, theaters, and an aqueduct. He built fortress-palaces at Masada, perched on a cliff above the Dead Sea, and at Herodium, a man-made mountain near Bethlehem where he would eventually be buried.

But his greatest project was the temple in Jerusalem. Herod essentially rebuilt the entire complex from the foundation up, expanding it to an enormous scale. The platform he constructed, supported by massive retaining walls, created the largest sacred precinct in the ancient world. The temple itself was covered in gold and white stone that blazed in the sunlight, visible from miles away. It took decades to complete, and it wasn't fully finished until long after Herod's death. Rabbis said that anyone who had not seen Herod's temple had never seen a truly beautiful building.

Why would a man like Herod build such a temple? Partly to win the loyalty of the Jewish people, who never fully accepted him. Partly to project power and prestige across the Roman world. And partly because Herod understood, as Machiavelli would later write, that a ruler should appear religious. The temple was his masterstroke of public relations.

But behind the golden façade was a man consumed by fear. Herod trusted no one. He murdered his beloved wife, Mariamme, on suspicion of disloyalty. He drowned his teenage brother-in-law, the high priest Aristobulus III, in a swimming pool because the young man was too popular. He executed three of his own sons when he suspected them of plotting against him. Caesar Augustus reportedly joked that it was safer to be Herod's pig than his son.

Herod appointed and removed high priests at will, turning the most sacred office in Judaism into a political tool. He created a new aristocracy loyal to himself, replacing the old families who might have challenged him. He built fortresses not just to defend his borders but to give himself places to run if his own people ever rose against him.

He was everything *The Prince* described: powerful, feared, strategic, and utterly without mercy.

A KINGDOM UNDER A SHADOW

By the end of Herod's reign, the Jewish world looked nothing like what the prophets had described and everything like what Machiavelli would have prescribed.

The temple was the most magnificent structure in the region, but it was controlled by priests that Herod handpicked. The nation had nominal independence, but every major decision required Rome's approval. The economy had expanded, but the tax burden crushed ordinary people. The land of Israel was larger than it had been in centuries, but it was held together by fear, not by faith.

When Herod died in 4 BC, the kingdom was divided among three of his surviving sons. None of them had their father's ability or his iron grip. Within a decade, the Romans would remove one of them and place Judea under direct Roman rule, governed by a series of Roman prefects. The most famous of these would be a man named Pontius Pilate.

The eagle had landed. Rome was in charge. And the Jewish people found themselves living under the most powerful empire the world had ever known, waiting for a king who would be everything Herod was not.

WHAT THIS MEANS FOR US

First, political power is never the answer to spiritual problems. The Hasmoneans sought power and it corrupted them.

Herod wielded absolute power and it consumed him. Rome had more power than any empire before it, and still it couldn't satisfy the deepest needs of the human heart. The kingdom Jesus came to establish would operate on entirely different principles, because the problems it was designed to solve were deeper than politics could reach.

Second, God's purposes cannot be stopped by human tyrants. Herod was brilliant, ruthless, and in complete control of his kingdom. But he couldn't prevent the birth of a baby in Bethlehem. He couldn't stop the purposes of a God whose plans were set before the foundation of the world. Every tyrant in this story—Antiochus, the Hasmoneans, Herod, Rome—thought they were in charge. None of them were.

Third, appearances can be deceiving. Herod built the most beautiful temple in the ancient world, but his heart was rotten. He appeared religious while being driven entirely by ambition and fear. Jesus would later warn his disciples about people who look impressive on the outside but are "whitewashed tombs" on the inside (Matthew 23:27). What matters to God is not what you build for show but what you are when nobody's looking.

Fourth, the darker the night, the brighter the star. The world Jesus was born into was dark. A paranoid king sat on the throne. A pagan empire ruled God's people. The priesthood was for sale. The poor were crushed. And yet it was into exactly this darkness that the light of the world arrived. God doesn't wait for conditions to improve before he acts. He acts precisely when things are at their worst.

TALKING POINTS

1. **Pompey walked into the holy of holies out of curiosity, violating the most sacred space in Jewish worship.** Why do you think this event was so traumatic for the Jewish people? What does it reveal about how Rome viewed the cultures it conquered?

2. **Herod built an extraordinary temple but murdered members of his own family.** How is it possible for someone to do impressive things for God's house while having a heart far from God? What warning does that carry for us?

3. **The Hasmonean brothers invited Rome in to settle their family dispute, and Rome never left.** Can you think of situations where inviting a powerful outside force to solve a problem created an even bigger one? What does this teach about being careful whose help you accept?

4. **Herod followed the Machiavellian playbook: eliminate rivals, appear religious, rule by fear.** Why is this kind of leadership so effective in the short term but so destructive in the long term? How does it contrast with the kind of leadership Jesus modeled?

5. **By the time Herod died, the Jewish people were living under Roman rule with a puppet king on the throne.** If you had been alive at that moment, what would you have been feeling? Would you have been hopeful that God was about to act, or would you have been tempted to give up? Why?

Rome rules. Herod's sons carve up his kingdom among themselves. Roman soldiers patrol the roads. Tax collectors squeeze the villages. The temple gleams in the sunlight, magnificent and hollow. And somewhere in the hill country of Judea, in synagogues and workshops and around dinner tables, ordinary people are still reading the Scriptures, still praying toward Jerusalem, still whispering the ancient promises to their children.

The eagle has landed. But the Lion of Judah is not dead. He's waiting.

Turn the page.

7

A PEOPLE DIVIDED

The 2024 film *Inside Out 2* picks up where the original left off. Riley is thirteen now, and her emotions are about to get complicated. Joy, Sadness, Anger, Fear, and Disgust have been running the show since she was little. They've figured out how to work together, more or less. But then Riley hits puberty, and a whole new crew of emotions shows up at headquarters: Anxiety, Envy, Ennui, and Embarrassment.

Suddenly, the control panel is crowded. Every emotion has a different idea about who Riley should be and how she should handle the pressures of growing up. Anxiety wants to plan for every possible disaster. Joy wants to stay positive. Anger wants to fight. Ennui can't be bothered with any of it. They're all inside the same person, all part of the same mind, but they're pulling in completely different directions. And the harder each emotion tries to take control, the more confused and fractured Riley becomes.

That movie is a surprisingly good picture of what happened to the Jewish people during the centuries between the Old and New Testaments. By the time Jesus was born, the Jewish nation wasn't a single, unified community with one vision of what it meant to follow God. It was a people being pulled apart from the inside by competing groups, each convinced that *their* understanding of faithfulness was the right one. These groups shared the same Scriptures, the same history, and the same God. But they couldn't agree on almost anything else.

If you've ever read the New Testament and wondered where the Pharisees and Sadducees came from, or why Jesus clashed with them, or why the Jewish leaders couldn't even agree among themselves about what to do with him, this chapter is your answer.

HOW DID ONE PEOPLE BECOME SO MANY?

The fracturing didn't happen overnight. It was the result of centuries of pressure.

As we've seen, the Jewish people spent generations being ruled by foreign empires: Persia, Greece, the Ptolemies, the Seleucids, and eventually Rome. Along the way, they faced constant questions about their identity. How Greek should they become? How much of the surrounding culture was acceptable? Who should lead the nation, and by what authority?

The Maccabean revolt unified the people for a brief, shining moment. But the Hasmonean dynasty that followed created new problems. When the Hasmoneans combined the offices of king and high priest in one family, it outraged people who believed only a descendant of David could be king and only a descendant of Zadok should be high priest. The more powerful the Hasmoneans became, the more opposition they generated.

By the time Rome arrived and Herod took the throne, the Jewish nation had splintered into distinct factions. Each group had a different diagnosis of what was wrong with the nation and a different prescription for how to fix it. They were all Jewish. They all believed in the God of Israel. But they couldn't have been more different in how they lived out that belief.

THE PHARISEES: GUARDIANS OF THE LAW

Of all the Jewish groups, the Pharisees are the ones most people recognize from the New Testament. Jesus argued with them constantly. But the Pharisees weren't the villains they're sometimes made out to be. They were deeply sincere people trying to solve a real problem.

The Pharisees believed that the key to Israel's survival was the law of Moses. If the people obeyed God's commands faithfully enough, God would bless and restore the nation. The problem, as the Pharisees saw it, was that the written law didn't cover every situation. Life was complicated. What counted as "work" on the Sabbath? Exactly how far could you walk? What if your animal fell into a ditch?

So the Pharisees developed what they called the Oral Law: an extensive set of additional rules and interpretations that built a fence around the written law. The idea was that if you kept all the extra rules, you'd never even get close to breaking the real ones. They saw themselves as teachers and protectors of ordinary people, and they operated through synagogues and schools rather than through the temple.

The Pharisees were populists. They worked among the common people, and the common people generally respected them. They believed in angels, in the resurrection of the dead, and in a coming age when God would set things right. Many of them believed a Messiah was coming.

But their extra rules could become suffocating. Jesus would later accuse them of loading people down with burdens they couldn't carry (Matthew 23:4) and of focusing so intensely on the details that they missed the heart of the law: justice, mercy, and faithfulness (Matthew 23:23). The Pharisees were trying to keep the nation holy. The danger was that their version of holiness became about control rather than love.

THE SADDUCEES: KEEPERS OF THE TEMPLE

The Sadducees were the aristocrats. They came from the wealthy priestly families who controlled the temple and dominated the ruling council in Jerusalem, the Sanhedrin. If the Pharisees were the populists, the Sadducees were the establishment.

The Sadducees took a very different approach to the law. They accepted only the written law of Moses, the first five books of the Bible, as fully authoritative. They rejected the Pharisees' Oral Law and many of the doctrines the Pharisees held dear. They did not believe in the resurrection of the dead. They did not believe in angels or demons. They believed that this life was all there was, and that faithfulness to God was about maintaining the temple worship and keeping the nation's institutions running smoothly.

Because they controlled the temple, the Sadducees had enormous power. The temple was the center of Jewish worship, the place where sacrifices were offered, and the economic engine of Jerusalem. Whoever controlled the temple controlled the nation's spiritual and financial life.

But that power came at a cost. The Sadducees were pragmatists. They cooperated with whatever foreign power was in charge, whether that was the Hasmoneans, Herod, or Rome. Their priority was stability. They wanted to keep the temple functioning, keep the sacrificial system going, and keep the peace with the occupying authorities. This made them deeply unpopular with ordinary people, who saw them as collaborators more interested in preserving their own status than in serving God's people.

When Jesus drove the money changers out of the temple and declared that the religious leaders had turned God's house into "a den of robbers" (Matthew 21:13), it was the Sadducees he was confronting. And it was the Sadducees who took the lead in arranging his arrest and trial.

THE ESSENES: THE ONES WHO WALKED AWAY

Not everyone wanted to fight for control of Jerusalem. Some Jews looked at the corruption of the priesthood, the political scheming, and the compromises with foreign powers, and decided the entire system was beyond saving. They walked away.

The Essenes withdrew from mainstream Jewish life. Some lived in small communities scattered across the countryside. Others went much further, forming a monastic community in the desert near the Dead Sea at a place called Qumran. They lived austere, disciplined lives devoted to prayer, study, and ritual purity. They shared their possessions. They followed strict rules about food, clothing, and daily conduct. They believed the temple in Jerusalem had been defiled by illegitimate priests and that its worship was no longer acceptable to God.

The Essenes were deeply committed to Scripture and produced a remarkable library of texts, including biblical manuscripts, commentaries, and writings about their own community. These texts, discovered in 1947 in caves near Qumran, are known as the Dead Sea Scrolls. They are among the most important archaeological discoveries in history, giving us a window into Jewish life and thought in the centuries just before Jesus.

The Essenes believed they were living in the last days. They expected God to intervene dramatically, to send a Messiah (or even two Messiahs, one kingly and one priestly), to destroy the wicked, and to establish a purified kingdom. Until that day came, their job was to remain pure, faithful, and separate from the corruption around them.

THE VIOLENT RESISTANCE

On the opposite end of the spectrum from the Essenes were those who believed the only answer to foreign oppression was the sword.

This wasn't a single organized group, at least not at first. It was more of a movement, a burning conviction shared by scattered bands of fighters and rebels who refused to accept Roman rule. They drew their inspiration from the Maccabees, who had taken up arms against the Seleucids and won. If God had delivered the nation through armed revolt before, maybe he would do it again.

These violent movements produced warlords and rebel leaders who launched uprisings, ambushed Roman patrols, and assassinated collaborators. They would eventually organize into groups like the Zealots and the Sicarii, the dagger-wielding assassins who blended into festival crowds and stabbed their political enemies in broad daylight.

For these fighters, paying taxes to Rome was a betrayal of God, because it meant acknowledging Caesar as lord instead of the God of Israel. Their passion was real. Their courage was extraordinary. But their methods brought devastating consequences. The violent resistance that simmered through the first century would eventually erupt into a full-scale war with Rome in AD 66, ending with the destruction of Jerusalem and the temple in AD 70.

It is worth noting that Jesus chose at least one disciple, Simon the Zealot (Matthew 10:4), from among those who sympathized with violent resistance. And two of the men crucified alongside Jesus were convicted rebels. The fact that Jesus drew people from this background and redirected their passion toward a different kind of kingdom says something profound about who he was and what he came to do.

THE FRACTURE LINES

So there it was. One nation, one God, one set of Scriptures, and at least four major visions of what faithfulness looked like.

The Sadducees said: Work within the system. Keep the temple running. Maintain order. For them, Judaism was about the institution.

The Pharisees said: Transform society from the ground up through obedience to the law. Build schools. Teach the people. For them, Judaism was about culture and devotion.

The Essenes said: The system is too corrupt to reform. Walk away. Stay pure. Wait for God to act. For them, Judaism was about personal holiness and hope.

The violent resistance said: Take up the sword. Throw out the Romans. Restore Jewish independence by force. For them, Judaism was about national identity and political freedom.

Each group believed it was right. Each believed the others were dangerously wrong. And the tension between them crackled through every synagogue, every marketplace, every family dinner table in the land of Israel.

This is the world Jesus walked into. And what's remarkable is that he didn't side with any of them. He shared the Pharisees' love of Scripture but rejected their crushing legalism. He honored the temple the Sadducees controlled but warned that it would be torn down. He valued the purity the Essenes sought but refused to withdraw from the broken world. He shared the passion for God's kingdom that drove the violent resistance but insisted that his kingdom would come through sacrifice, not swords.

Jesus didn't come to pick a faction. He came to do something none of them had imagined.

WHAT THIS MEANS FOR US

First, people who love God can disagree deeply about what faithfulness looks like. The Pharisees, Sadducees, Essenes, and others all claimed to follow the God of Israel. Most of them were sincere. But they came to radically different conclusions about how to live. That should make us humble about our own certainty and careful about how we treat people who read the same Bible but reach different conclusions about how to apply it.

Second, every group has blind spots. The Pharisees couldn't see that their extra rules were becoming a burden. The Sadducees couldn't see that their compromises were corroding the faith. The Essenes couldn't see that withdrawal abandoned the people who needed them most. The Zealots couldn't see that violence would destroy what they were trying to save. Every approach to faithfulness carries the risk of overemphasis. Knowing your own blind spots is one of the most valuable things you can learn.

Third, institutions matter, but they aren't the point. The temple, the Sanhedrin, the synagogues, the schools—these were all important. But when they became ends in themselves, when people cared more about the institution than about the God the institution was supposed to serve, everything went wrong. The same danger exists for churches today. The building, the programs, the traditions—these are tools, not goals. The goal is always God and his people.

Fourth, Jesus transcended every category. He didn't fit neatly into any existing group, and that frustrated everyone. The Pharisees wanted him to be stricter. The Sadducees wanted him to go away. The Essenes probably wondered why he spent so much time with sinners. The Zealots wanted him to pick up a sword. Jesus refused to be captured by any human agenda because he was carrying out a divine one. That's still how he operates. The moment you think you've got Jesus figured out and filed into your category, he'll surprise you.

TALKING POINTS

1. **Each Jewish faction had a different vision of what it meant to be faithful to God.** Which group's approach do you

most relate to, and why? Which group's mistakes seem most familiar to you?

2. **The Pharisees added extra rules to God's law with good intentions, trying to help people avoid sin.** How can good intentions lead to legalism? What's the difference between helpful guidelines and burdensome rules?

3. **The Sadducees cooperated with foreign powers to keep the peace and maintain the temple.** When is compromise wise, and when does it cross the line into unfaithfulness? How do you tell the difference?

4. **The Essenes walked away from a corrupt system rather than try to fix it.** Do you think that was the right decision? When is it appropriate to withdraw from something broken, and when should you stay and fight for change?

5. **Jesus didn't fit into any of the existing groups. He challenged every faction.** Why do you think that made him dangerous to all of them? What does it tell us about how God's kingdom works compared to human expectations?

The Jewish people are fractured and waiting. The Pharisees are teaching in the synagogues. The Sadducees are running the temple. The Essenes are praying in the desert. Rebels are sharpening their swords in the hills. And all of them, in their own way, are asking the same question: When will God finally act?

The answer is closer than any of them realize. But first, we need to understand the new institutions that grew up during these centuries and changed the shape of Jewish worship forever.

Turn the page.

8

A NEW WAY TO WORSHIP

Have you ever been away from your home church? Maybe you were at camp, or on vacation, or visiting family in another state. Sunday morning came, and the building where you usually worship was hundreds of miles away. The preacher you're used to hearing wasn't there. The songs were different. The people were strangers.

But someone opened a Bible. Someone prayed. And even though the building, the routine, and the familiar faces were all missing, something essential was still there. God's word was still God's word, no matter where you read it.

Now imagine that feeling lasting not for a weekend but for a lifetime. Imagine that you and your family live five hundred miles from the only place where God can be properly worshiped. You might make the journey once in your life, maybe twice if you're lucky. But most weeks, most months, most years, the temple in Jerusalem is just a distant idea, a place you pray toward but never see.

That was reality for millions of Jewish people during the centuries between the Old and New Testaments. As the Jewish population scattered across the Mediterranean world, from Egypt to Syria to Asia Minor to Rome itself, a practical question demanded an answer: How do you worship God when you can't get to the temple?

The answer changed everything. It changed how Jews practiced their faith. It changed how they organized their communities. And centuries later, it gave the early church a ready-made network for spreading the gospel across the known world.

WHEN THE TEMPLE WASN'T ENOUGH

The temple in Jerusalem was the center of Jewish worship. It was the place where sacrifices were offered, where priests served, where God's presence was understood to dwell in a special way. The entire sacrificial system described in Leviticus depended on the temple. You couldn't offer a burnt offering in your backyard. You couldn't sacrifice a lamb for Passover in Alexandria. For the rituals that defined Jewish worship, you had to go to Jerusalem.

But by the third century BC, most Jews didn't live anywhere near Jerusalem. The Babylonian exile had scattered the Jewish people across Mesopotamia. Alexander's conquests and the policies of the Ptolemies had spread them further, especially into Egypt. By the time of Jesus, there were Jewish communities in virtually every major city in the Roman world. Some estimates suggest that more Jews lived outside the land of Israel than inside it.

These diaspora or "dispersed" communities faced a real dilemma. They couldn't participate in temple worship on a regular basis. The journey was too long, too expensive, and too dangerous for most families to make more than once or twice in a lifetime. Were they supposed to just do without? Were they cut off from God because geography separated them from his house?

The answer, born out of necessity and shaped by centuries of development, was the synagogue.

THE RISE OF THE SYNAGOGUE

The word "synagogue" simply means "gathering." In its earliest form, it wasn't a building at all. It was a group of people coming together to pray, read Scripture, and encourage one another in their faith.

The earliest evidence of dedicated gathering places comes from Egypt in the third century BC, where they were called "prayer houses." Jewish communities built these meeting spaces so they would have a place to read the Scriptures, pray together, and store their precious scrolls. The earliest known prayer house dates to the reign of Ptolemy III, around 240 BC, and stood on about two and a half acres of land outside a city in the Egyptian countryside, beside a canal that provided access to water.

These prayer houses served several purposes at once. They were places of worship where the community gathered on the Sabbath to hear Scripture read and explained. They were schools where children could learn to read using the sacred texts. They were community centers where Jewish travelers could find hospitality. And they were safe houses for the scrolls themselves, which were expensive to produce and irreplaceable.

Over time, this model spread. As Pharisees developed schools throughout the land of Israel, and as Jewish communities continued to grow across the diaspora, dedicated synagogue buildings became increasingly common. By the first century BC, synagogues could be found in every significant Jewish community, both inside and outside the land of Israel.

A synagogue from this period has been excavated in Jerusalem itself. A dedicatory inscription tells us it was built by a man named Theodotos, whose father and grandfather had also led the synagogue before him. The inscription says it was built "for the reading of the law and the teaching of the commandments," along with guest rooms and water facilities for travelers from abroad. Even in Jerusalem, where the temple was right there, people wanted a place to study Scripture and learn.

WHAT HAPPENED ON THE SABBATH

Walk into a first-century synagogue on a Sabbath morning and here's roughly what you would have experienced.

The building was simple. Benches lined the walls. At one end sat a special chest, called an ark, that held the scrolls of Scripture. There was a raised platform where the reader would stand, and a prominent seat near the front, sometimes called "Moses' seat," where the leader or a distinguished teacher would sit.

The service centered on Scripture. A portion of the law of Moses was read aloud, working through the text systematically so that the entire law was covered over a set period. A reading from the Prophets followed. Since many Jews in the diaspora spoke Greek rather than the original languages, the readings were often translated or paraphrased so people could understand.

After the readings, someone would stand to teach. This wasn't limited to one official leader. If a recognized teacher or visiting rabbi was present, he might be invited to offer instruction. This is how Jesus launched his public ministry. In Luke 4, he walked into the synagogue in Nazareth on the Sabbath, was handed the scroll of Isaiah, read from it, sat down in the teacher's seat, and declared, "Today this Scripture has been fulfilled in your hearing." The synagogue was the platform for his announcement.

Prayers were offered, including blessings and petitions that followed established patterns. The service was participatory in a way that temple worship was not. At the temple, priests performed the rituals while the people watched from a distance. At the synagogue, ordinary people read, discussed, and engaged with the word of God directly.

This was a revolution. For the first time in Jewish history, the study of Scripture became the centerpiece of regular community worship. The temple was still revered as the sacred center, the place of sacrifice, the dwelling of God. But the synagogue put God's word into the hands and ears of ordinary people every single week.

THE SCRIBES AND TEACHERS

The rise of the synagogue created a need for a new kind of spiritual leader. The temple had priests. The synagogue needed teachers.

Before the exile, Israel's spiritual life had been guided by priests, prophets, and kings. By the time we reach the centuries before Jesus, the kings were gone, the prophets had fallen silent, and the priests were focused on the temple rituals. A new class of leaders emerged to fill the gap: scribes and teachers of the law.

These were men devoted to studying, copying, and interpreting Scripture. They spent their lives learning the sacred texts and teaching them to others. The most respected among them earned the title "rabbi," meaning "great one" or "master." They attracted students, called disciples, who would follow them, learn their methods of interpretation, and eventually become teachers themselves.

Two rabbis from the generation just before Jesus became especially famous: Hillel and Shammai. Hillel was known for a more generous, flexible approach to interpreting the law. Shammai was stricter. Their students formed rival schools that debated nearly every point of the law. When the Gospels record arguments about Sabbath rules, divorce, and the greatest commandment, these debates were happening against the backdrop of the Hillel-Shammai rivalry that had been shaping Jewish thought for decades.

The apostle Paul was trained in this tradition. He studied under Gamaliel, the grandson of Hillel, one of the most respected teachers in Jerusalem (Acts 22:3). When Paul reasoned from the Scriptures in synagogues across the Roman world (Acts 17:2), he was using the skills he had learned in this very system.

THE SANHEDRIN

While the synagogue shaped local community life, the Sanhedrin governed the nation at the highest level. The Sanhedrin was the supreme council in Jerusalem, a body of seventy-one members that included the high priest, leading priests, elders, and scribes from both the Sadducee and Pharisee parties.

The Sanhedrin served as a combination of supreme court and legislative body. It ruled on matters of religious law, settled disputes, and exercised authority over the temple. Under Roman rule, it retained significant power over internal Jewish affairs, though it could not carry out the death penalty without Roman approval (which is why the Jewish leaders had to bring Jesus before Pilate).

The composition of the Sanhedrin shifted over the centuries. Under the Hasmoneans, the Sadducees had dominated. Under Herod and the Romans, the balance shifted as Pharisees gained more seats. By the time of Jesus, both parties were represented, which meant that the Sanhedrin was itself a place of constant tension and disagreement. The trial of Jesus exposed exactly this dynamic, as the council struggled to find charges that would stick and witnesses who would agree (Mark 14:55–59).

GOD WAS BUILDING SOMETHING

Step back and look at what happened during these centuries, and a remarkable picture emerges.

Without any prophet commanding it, without any miracle announcing it, a system developed that would become one of the most important structures in all of religious history. By the time Jesus began his ministry, there was a synagogue in virtually every Jewish community in the known world. Each one had copies of the Scriptures. Each one had teachers who could explain them. Each one gathered every Sabbath to read God's word and pray.

And when the gospel began to spread, where did the apostles go first? The synagogue. In city after city, Paul walked into the local synagogue, opened the Scriptures, and proclaimed that Jesus was the Messiah (Acts 13:14–15; 17:1–2; 18:4). The synagogue network gave the early church a ready-made audience of people who already knew the Scriptures, already believed in one God, and were already waiting for the Messiah. It also gave them access to the "Godfearers," Gentiles who were attracted to Jewish worship and attended synagogue services without fully converting. Many of these Godfearers became some of the earliest non-Jewish Christians (Acts 13:43; 17:4).

None of this was planned by any human committee. No prophet stood up and said, "Build synagogues in every city so the gospel can travel through them someday." It grew organically out of the practical needs of scattered communities trying to stay faithful to God far from the temple.

But God was in it. Quietly, providentially, he was building the infrastructure that his Son and his church would use to change the world.

WHAT THIS MEANS FOR US

First, worship doesn't require a building. The synagogue started as a gathering, not a structure. People came together to read Scripture, pray, and encourage one another wherever they could find space. The building came later. What mattered was the word, the community, and the presence of God among his people. That's still what matters. A church is not a building. It's the people of God gathered around the word of God.

Second, Scripture must be accessible to everyone. The synagogue put the word of God into the ears and hands of ordinary people every week. It wasn't locked away in a temple where only priests could access it. It was read aloud, explained, and discussed in the common language of the community. When God's word is kept from ordinary people, faith suffers. When it's made available, faith grows.

Third, faithful systems outlast the people who build them. The men and women who established the first prayer houses in Egypt had no idea they were creating a network that would carry the gospel across the Roman Empire. They were just trying to stay faithful. But their quiet, practical obedience created something that lasted for centuries and served God's purposes in ways they never imagined. The faithful systems you build today—the habits of worship, study, and community—may serve purposes you'll never see.

Fourth, God builds slowly what he intends to use powerfully. The synagogue system took centuries to develop. It grew gradually, organically, without fanfare. But when the moment came, when the gospel needed a delivery system, the infrastructure was already in place. God is patient. He builds things over long stretches of time that look unremarkable in the moment but prove essential when the time is right. Trust the slow work of God.

TALKING POINTS

1. **The synagogue developed because Jews who lived far from the temple needed a way to worship.** What does this tell you about God's willingness to meet people where they are, rather than requiring them to come to one specific place?

2. **Synagogue worship centered on reading and discussing Scripture, while temple worship centered on sacrifice and ritual.** How are these two approaches to worship different? How do they complement each other?

3. **The scribes and rabbis became influential because they devoted their lives to studying and teaching God's word.** What does their example teach us about the importance of knowing Scripture deeply? How can you grow in your own knowledge of the Bible?

4. **Paul used the synagogue network to spread the gospel across the Roman Empire.** What are the "synagogue networks" of our own time, the existing systems and communities that the gospel can travel through?

5. **The synagogue system grew gradually over centuries without any prophet commanding it.** Can you think of other examples where God worked through ordinary, unplanned developments to accomplish extraordinary things?

The Jewish people have developed a way to worship that doesn't depend on a single building in a single city. Synagogues dot the landscape from Jerusalem to Rome. Scribes and rabbis teach in every community. The Scriptures are being read, discussed, and cherished in homes and gathering places across the known world. The infrastructure is in place.

But all these changes, all these developments, all these centuries of preparation, are pointing toward one thing: the unshakable conviction, shared by every faction and every community, that God is going to act. The hope that kept burning through every crisis and every conquest is about to reach its breaking point.

Turn the page.

9

THE HOPE THAT WOULDN'T DIE

Steven Spielberg's 1977 film *Close Encounters of the Third Kind* tells the story of Roy Neary, an ordinary electrician in Indiana who sees something he can't explain: strange lights in the sky, a force that shakes his truck and burns one side of his face. From that moment on, Roy is consumed by a vision. He keeps seeing the shape of a flat-topped mountain in his mind. He sculpts it out of mashed potatoes at dinner. He builds it out of mud and garbage in his living room. His family thinks he's lost his mind.

But Roy can't let go. Something is coming. He doesn't know what, and he can't prove it, but the conviction has taken root so deeply that nothing can shake it. He abandons his job, his routine, his comfort. He drives across the country to find the mountain he keeps seeing. And when he finally gets there, when the lights appear again, when the enormous spacecraft descends from the clouds, the truth is revealed: he was right all along. Something extraordinary was coming. And it was bigger and more beautiful than anyone could have imagined.

For centuries, the Jewish people lived with that kind of consuming conviction. They believed, with every fiber of their being, that God was going to act. That a deliverer was coming. That the kingdoms of the world would give way to the kingdom of God. That the promises spoken by the prophets, some of them already hundreds of years old, had not expired and would not fail.

The evidence didn't support it. They were a conquered people under foreign rule. Their temple had been desecrated and rebuilt, their leaders were corrupt, and the great empires of the world paid them almost no attention. Every rational calculation said the dream was dead.

But the hope wouldn't die. It burned hotter with every passing generation. And by the time a baby was born in Bethlehem, that hope had reached a temperature no one could ignore.

THE PROMISES THEY CLUNG TO

The messianic hope of the Jewish people wasn't a vague wish that things would get better. It was rooted in specific promises God had made through the prophets, promises recorded in Scripture that the people read and discussed in their synagogues every Sabbath.

God had told Abraham that through his descendants, all the nations of the earth would be blessed (Genesis 12:3). He had promised David that one of his descendants would sit on an eternal throne (2 Samuel 7:12–16). The prophets had spoken of a coming king who would reign with justice, a servant who would suffer for the sins of the people, a day when God would pour out his Spirit and make all things new.

Isaiah had written about a child who would be called "Wonderful Counselor, Mighty God, Everlasting Father,

Prince of Peace," whose government and peace would never end (Isaiah 9:6–7). Jeremiah had promised a new covenant, written not on stone but on human hearts (Jeremiah 31:31–34). Ezekiel had described dry bones coming back to life, a picture of national resurrection (Ezekiel 37). Daniel had seen a vision of "one like a son of man" approaching the throne of God and receiving an everlasting kingdom that would never be destroyed (Daniel 7:13–14).

These weren't obscure footnotes. They were the heartbeat of Jewish faith. Every time a foreign army marched through Jerusalem, every time a corrupt leader exploited the people, every time the gap between God's promises and present reality grew wider, the Jewish people went back to these texts and said: God promised. God doesn't lie. Therefore, it must still be coming.

WHAT THEY WERE WAITING FOR

But what exactly were they expecting? This is where it gets complicated, because different groups had different visions of what God's intervention would look like.

Most Jews expected a Messiah, literally an "anointed one," a king descended from David who would liberate Israel from foreign oppression, restore the kingdom, and reign with justice and power. This was the dominant expectation, and it's the one that shaped how people responded to Jesus. When crowds waved palm branches and shouted "Hosanna to the Son of David" as Jesus entered Jerusalem, they were invoking this hope. They wanted a warrior king who would drive out the Romans the way David had conquered the Philistines.

Some groups, especially the Essenes, expected not one Messiah but two: a kingly Messiah from the line of David and a priestly Messiah from the line of Aaron. They believed the proper order of things required both a righteous king and a pure priest, since the corruption of both offices had been at the heart of Israel's problems.

Others focused less on a human deliverer and more on God himself intervening directly. They expected a dramatic, cosmic event: the heavens opening, angels descending, the dead rising, evil being judged, and a new age dawning in which God's rule would be visible and unchallenged. This expectation was fueled by a particular kind of literature that flourished during the intertestamental period.

THE LITERATURE OF BURNING HOPE

When the prophetic voice fell silent after Malachi, it didn't mean that people stopped writing about God's purposes. Jewish writers during the intertestamental period produced a remarkable body of literature that expressed their hopes, their anguish, and their unshakable conviction that God would act.

The most important category of this writing is called apocalyptic literature, from a word meaning "unveiling" or "revelation." These writings claimed to pull back the curtain on hidden realities: the spiritual forces behind earthly empires, the architecture of heaven, the timetable of God's plan, and the events that would unfold at the end of the age.

Apocalyptic literature was packed with vivid, strange imagery: beasts rising from the sea, angels doing battle, thrones of fire, numbers with hidden meanings. To modern readers, this imagery can seem bizarre. But to people steeped in the Old Testament, the symbols were recognizable. Beasts represented empires. Horns represented rulers. Numbers like seven (completeness), twelve (God's people), and a thousand (an overwhelming fullness) carried specific meaning.

The book of Daniel, written centuries earlier during the Babylonian exile, became the template. Daniel's visions of successive empires being crushed by God's eternal kingdom (Daniel 2, 7) provided the framework that later writers built on. During the intertestamental period, works like 1 Enoch, the Psalms of Solomon, and others expanded on Daniel's themes, applying them to the current crises the Jewish people faced.

These writings were not Scripture. They were not the word of God delivered through prophets. But they reflected the deep conviction of faithful Jews that the God who had spoken through the prophets was still sovereign over history, still moving toward the fulfillment of his promises, and still worthy of trust even when centuries passed without visible evidence of his action.

The core message of this literature was simple and fierce: the present evil age will end. God will establish his kingdom. The righteous will be vindicated. The wicked will be judged. And it could happen at any moment.

NEW IDEAS, ANCIENT ROOTS

The centuries of waiting also produced theological developments that would become central to the New Testament. These ideas didn't appear out of thin air. They grew from seeds already planted in the Old Testament, watered by centuries of reflection and experience.

Resurrection became a firm belief for many Jews during this period. The idea that God would raise the dead appears in the Old Testament (Isaiah 26:19; Daniel 12:2), but it was during the intertestamental period that resurrection became a widely held conviction. The martyrs under Antiochus IV had died believing God would raise them to new life (2 Maccabees 7). The Pharisees made resurrection a central doctrine. The Sadducees rejected it, which is why they tried to trap Jesus with a question about marriage and resurrection (Matthew 22:23–33). By the time Jesus stood at the tomb of Lazarus and said, "I am the resurrection and the life" (John 11:25), he was speaking into a world where resurrection was already a matter of fierce debate.

Final judgment took sharper focus during this period. The Old Testament prophets had spoken of "the day of the Lord," a time of divine reckoning. Jewish thinkers during these centuries developed this into a more detailed picture of a final judgment at the end of history, where every person would stand before God and give account. This is the backdrop for Jesus' parables about sheep and goats, wheat and weeds, servants who invested and servants who buried their talents.

Angels and demons became more prominent in Jewish thinking. The Old Testament mentions angels, but the intertestamental period saw a much more developed understanding of spiritual beings, both good and evil, operating behind the scenes of human history. This is the world Jesus stepped into when he cast out demons and declared that he had seen "Satan fall like lightning from heaven" (Luke 10:18).

A WORLD HOLDING ITS BREATH

By the time Jesus was born, messianic expectation in the Jewish world had reached an intensity that is hard to overstate.

The people had been waiting for centuries. They had endured Persian rule, Greek rule, the Maccabean uprising and its disillusioning aftermath, the corrupt Hasmonean dynasty, and now the Roman occupation under the shadow of Herod the Great, a man who murdered members of his own family and would slaughter the infants of Bethlehem without a second thought.

Every crisis made the hope sharper. Every oppressor made the longing fiercer. The worse things got, the more people believed that God's intervention must be close. The world was too broken. Evil was too powerful. The gap between what God had promised and what the people experienced was too vast to endure forever. Something had to give.

And then, quietly, it did.

An elderly priest named Zechariah was burning incense in the temple when an angel appeared and told him his wife would bear a son who would "make ready a people prepared for the Lord" (Luke 1:17). A young woman named Mary was told she would conceive a child who would sit on the throne of David and reign over a kingdom that would never end (Luke 1:32–33). Shepherds in a field near Bethlehem heard an army of angels announce peace on earth. An old man named Simeon held a baby in the temple courts and said, "My eyes have seen your salvation, which you have prepared in the sight of all nations" (Luke 2:30–31).

After four hundred years of silence, God spoke again.

And what he said was not a battle plan or a political strategy. It was a name.

Jesus.

The hope had not died. It had been waiting for exactly this.

WHAT THIS MEANS FOR US

First, God's promises don't have expiration dates. The Jewish people waited centuries for the fulfillment of what the prophets had spoken. Generations lived and died without seeing it. But God was not late. He was working on a timetable that only he could see. When you're waiting for God to act, the delay doesn't mean the promise is dead. It means the timing isn't yours to control.

Second, the darkest moments can be the closest to dawn. Messianic hope burned hottest when conditions were worst. Under Antiochus, under Herod, under Rome, the conviction that God was about to act didn't weaken. It intensified. If you're in a season of suffering and it seems like things can't get any worse, you may be closer to God's intervention than you think. Don't let the darkness convince you that the light isn't coming.

Third, God's answer is usually bigger than our expectations. The Jews expected a military king. God sent a baby in a feeding trough. They expected an army. God sent shepherds and angels. They expected political liberation from Rome. God offered liberation from sin and death. God's answer to human suffering wasn't smaller than what people hoped for. It was so much bigger that most of them didn't recognize it when it arrived. Be careful about insisting that God answer your prayers in the exact form you've imagined. His imagination is better than yours.

Fourth, knowing the promises keeps hope alive. The Jewish people survived centuries of waiting because they kept reading the Scriptures. They kept reciting the promises. They kept telling their children about the God who had delivered their ancestors and sworn to deliver them. Hope doesn't survive on feelings. It survives on the word of God. If your hope is fading, go back to the promises. Read them again. They haven't changed, and neither has the God who made them.

TALKING POINTS

1. **The Jewish people waited for centuries for God to fulfill the promises made through the prophets.** What do you think that kind of waiting does to faith? Does it strengthen it or weaken it, and why?

2. **Different groups had different ideas about what God's intervention would look like: a warrior king, a priestly reformer, a cosmic event.** Why do you think people's expectations of God are shaped so much by their circumstances? How do your own circumstances shape what you expect from God?

3. **Apocalyptic literature used vivid imagery like beasts, thrones, and angels to describe spiritual realities behind earthly events.** Why do you think people were drawn to this kind of writing during times of suffering? What comfort does it offer to believe that there's a bigger story behind what you can see?

4. **Many Jews expected God to act through military power and political liberation. Instead, Jesus came as a servant who conquered through sacrifice.** Why is it so hard for people to accept a God who works through weakness rather than strength?

5. The chapter says "hope doesn't survive on feelings; it survives on the word of God." Do you agree with that? What practices or habits help you hold onto hope when circumstances are difficult and God seems silent?

The promises have been spoken. The hope has burned for centuries. The synagogues are full of people reading the Scriptures and longing for the day when God will finally keep his word. And now, in the fullness of time, all the pieces are in place. The language is ready. The roads are built. The communities are established. The expectations are at their peak.

Everything the centuries between the Testaments have produced—every empire, every crisis, every institution, every idea—is about to converge on a single moment in a small town in Judea.

Turn the page.

10

THE STAGE IS SET

Have you ever been on a road trip so long that you started to wonder if you'd ever get there? The first hour is exciting. The second is tolerable. By the fourth or fifth, you've run out of things to look at. The landscape blurs together. You ask "are we there yet?" and the answer is always the same: not yet. You start to wonder if the destination is even real. Maybe you'll be in this car forever. Maybe nothing is waiting at the end of the road.

And then, without warning, you see the sign. The exit. The skyline. You're there. And suddenly everything you drove through—the flat stretches, the detours, the gas station stops in towns you'll never visit again—all of it makes sense. It was all part of getting here.

The Jewish people had been on a road trip for four hundred years. And everything we've covered in this book, every empire, every crisis, every development, was the road. The Persian period, Alexander's conquests, the Ptolemies and Seleucids, the Maccabean revolt, the Hasmonean dynasty, Rome's arrival, Herod's throne, the rise of synagogues, the fracturing of the nation, the burning hope for a Messiah—all of it was the landscape between the last page of the Old Testament and the first page of the New.

Now it's time to see where the road was leading all along.

THE WORLD IN PLACE

Step back and look at the world as it existed around the year 5 BC, and something remarkable emerges. Without anyone planning it, without any committee arranging it, the pieces had fallen into place for an event that would change everything.

There was one language. Greek had become the common tongue of the Mediterranean world. A fisherman in Galilee and a merchant in Rome might not share a culture, but they could communicate. When the gospel needed to be preached, written down, and carried from city to city, the language was already there.

There was one road system. Rome had built an extraordinary network of roads connecting the entire empire. These were originally built to move armies quickly. But they would also carry missionaries, letters, and the message of a crucified and risen King to the farthest corners of the known world. Paul could travel from Jerusalem to Rome on roads that didn't exist two centuries earlier.

There was one peace. The Roman Empire, for all its brutality, had imposed a stability across the Mediterranean world that hadn't existed before. The constant wars between rival kingdoms had mostly ceased. Travel was safer than it had been in centuries. Bandits still roamed the highways, but the basic infrastructure of a connected, relatively stable world was in place. Historians call this the Pax Romana, the Roman peace.

It was enforced by the sword, but it created conditions in which a peaceful message could spread.

And there was one network. Synagogues dotted every major city in the empire. Each one had copies of the Scriptures, teachers who could explain them, and a community of people who already believed in one God and were already waiting for a Messiah. When the apostles began to carry the gospel, they didn't have to start from scratch. The infrastructure was built. The audience was assembled. The Scriptures were being read every Sabbath in the very language the New Testament would be written in.

None of this was coincidence. None of it was random. God had spent four hundred years quietly arranging the world for the arrival of his Son.

THE MAN ON THE THRONE

But the world Jesus was born into wasn't just convenient. It was dark.

Herod the Great sat on the throne of Judea. He was a brilliant builder and a ruthless tyrant. He had renovated the Jerusalem temple into the largest sacred complex in the ancient world, a structure so magnificent that people traveled from across the empire just to see it. Rabbis said, "Whoever has not seen Herod's building has never seen a beautiful building."

But Herod was also a monster. He had murdered his own wife, Mariamme, whom he deeply loved, out of jealous paranoia. He executed three of his own sons because he suspected them of plotting against him. Caesar Augustus reportedly quipped that it was safer to be Herod's pig than Herod's son, since as a nominal Jew, Herod wouldn't eat pork but had no problem killing his children.

Herod wasn't a descendant of David. He wasn't even fully Jewish. He was an Idumean, a foreigner whose family had converted to Judaism. He held his throne by Roman permission and by terror. The man who sat on the throne that rightly belonged to a descendant of David was an outsider, a pretender, a violent fraud.

When Matthew tells us that wise men from the east came looking for "the one born king of the Jews" and that Herod was "disturbed" by the news (Matthew 2:2–3), you now understand why. Herod knew the messianic hopes. He knew the Jewish people were waiting for a real king, a legitimate heir to David's throne. And he knew that when that king appeared, Herod's dynasty was finished.

His response was exactly what you would expect from the man he was. He ordered the slaughter of every male child in Bethlehem under two years old (Matthew 2:16). This act of infanticide is consistent with everything we know about Herod historically. This was a man who killed his own sons. Killing the sons of strangers would have cost him nothing.

THE FRACTURED NATION

Beneath Herod's throne, the Jewish nation was as divided as it had ever been.

The Sadducees controlled the temple and cooperated with whatever government kept them in power. The Pharisees ran the synagogues and schools, pressing their vision of strict obedience on the common people. The Essenes had withdrawn to the desert, praying and waiting for God to act. Zealots and revolutionaries sharpened their daggers and dreamed of armed revolt. And ordinary people, the farmers and fishermen and carpenters of Galilee and Judea, ground out their lives under heavy taxation, trying to stay faithful to a God who seemed to have gone quiet a very long time ago.

The Sanhedrin in Jerusalem was a battleground between Sadducees and Pharisees. The high priesthood was no longer an office held for life by the rightful heir. It was a political appointment, handed out by Herod to men he could control. The sacred office that God had established through Moses had become a tool of a foreign king who answered to Rome.

The gap between rich and poor was staggering. The temple economy enriched the priestly aristocracy while ordinary people struggled to pay their tithes, their taxes to Rome, and their taxes to Herod. Tax collectors, working for the system, squeezed the population with the same ruthlessness that had characterized the Ptolemaic tax farmers centuries earlier.

This was not the kingdom of God. This was not what the prophets had described. The promises were still unclaimed. The throne was still empty, at least in the eyes of anyone who took the Scriptures seriously.

THE FULLNESS OF TIME

The apostle Paul would later write a sentence that compresses four hundred years of history into a single breath: "When the fullness of time had come, God sent forth his Son" (Galatians 4:4).

The fullness of time. Not a random moment. Not an accident. The moment when every thread God had been weaving came together.

The Greek language was ready. The Roman roads were built. The synagogue network was in place. The Scriptures had been translated, studied, debated, and cherished. The messianic hope was burning at its hottest. The world was connected, stable enough for a message to travel, and broken enough to know it needed saving.

And into that world, in a town called Bethlehem, a baby was born. Not in a palace. Not with an army. Not with the fanfare the world expected. He was born to a teenage girl and a carpenter, laid in a feeding trough because there was no room for them anywhere else.

Luke tells us that an angel appeared to shepherds in the fields outside town and said, "Do not be afraid. I bring you good news that will cause great joy for all the people. Today in the town of David a Savior has been born to you; he is the Messiah, the Lord" (Luke 2:10–11).

Today. In the town of David. A Savior. The Messiah. The Lord.

Every word of that announcement was loaded with four centuries of meaning. "The town of David" pointed back to the ancient promise. "Savior" answered the cry of a people who had been conquered, scattered, and oppressed. "Messiah" was the word generations had whispered in the dark, the hope they had refused to surrender. "Lord" was a direct challenge to every Caesar, every Herod, every human pretender who had ever claimed ultimate authority over God's people.

And it was announced not to the Sanhedrin, not to the Pharisees, not to the priests, not to the Sadducees, not to the Essenes, not to the Zealots, but to shepherds. Ordinary, unimportant, working-class men watching their flocks in the middle of the night.

God's answer to four hundred years of waiting arrived not on a warhorse but in a manger. Not with a sword but with swaddling cloths. Not to the powerful but to the forgotten.

WHAT THIS MEANS FOR US

First, God is never late. Four hundred years of silence felt like forever to the people who lived through it. But God wasn't behind schedule. He was working through every century, every crisis, every cultural shift, preparing the world for the moment when his Son would step into it. When God seems slow, he is not idle. He is precise.

Second, God's plan is bigger than any human faction. The Pharisees thought they had the answer. So did the Sadducees, the Essenes, and the Zealots. Each group built an entire worldview around its own vision of what God should do. None of them got it right. Jesus didn't validate any faction's agenda. He fulfilled God's agenda, which was bigger, wider, deeper, and more beautiful than anything any of them had imagined. Be humble about your own plans for what God should do. His plans are better.

Third, God uses everything. Pagan empires. Greek philosophers. Roman engineers. Corrupt kings. Scattered exiles. Tax farmers. All of them, without knowing it, played a role in preparing the way for the gospel. God is not limited to working through people who love him. He can use anyone, anything, and any circumstance to accomplish his purposes. Nothing in your life is wasted if God is sovereign over it.

Fourth, the story isn't over. The intertestamental period ended with the birth of Jesus, but the story of God's work in the world didn't. The same God who worked through four centuries of silence is still working today. The same promises that sustained the Jewish people through exile, persecution, and empire are the same promises that sustain you. And the same Jesus who was born in Bethlehem, who lived and died and rose again, is still alive, still reigning, and still calling people to follow him.

TALKING POINTS

1. **Paul wrote that Jesus came in "the fullness of time."** After studying the intertestamental period, what do you think that phrase means? How did the centuries before Jesus prepare the world for his arrival?

2. **God announced the birth of the Messiah to shepherds, not to religious leaders or political authorities.** What does that tell you about the kind of kingdom Jesus came to establish? Why do you think God chose the audience he did?

3. **Herod tried to destroy the newborn Messiah, just as Antiochus had tried to destroy the Jewish faith and Pharaoh had tried to destroy the Israelite children.** What pattern do you see in these stories? What does it tell you about how the world responds to what God is doing?

4. **The Jewish people expected a political and military Messiah, but God sent a baby in a manger.** How do you think the people we've studied in this book—the Pharisees, Sadducees, Essenes, and Zealots—would have reacted to the kind of Messiah Jesus turned out to be?

5. **Look back over everything you've learned about the intertestamental period.** What surprised you the most? How has understanding this period changed the way you read the New Testament?

Four hundred years of silence. Four hundred years of empires rising and falling, of faithful people holding on, of promises spoken and not yet kept.

And then, in the quietest way imaginable, God broke the silence.

Not with thunder from a mountaintop. Not with plagues against an empire. Not with a prophet's voice ringing through the temple courts. He broke it with the cry of a newborn in a borrowed stable, wrapped in rags, held by a young mother who had been told by an angel that her son would sit on David's throne forever.

The centuries between the Testaments were never silent. God was at work in every one of them, bending history, shaping nations, preserving his people, and arranging the world for this one moment. The road was long. The wait was brutal. But every mile of it was leading here.

The stage was set. The king had come. And nothing would ever be the same.